College & Real Life Skills for Success
AFTER GRADUATION

Deborah Insel

- Welcome to college! Get started & get focused
- Make a successful social, academic & emotional transition to college
- Manage your time
- Manage your independence & personal responsibilities
- Manage your money & your financial aid
- Create a "success network" for yourself
- Tips for students who are working, commuting or parenting

Reach for College! ®

© Deborah Insel 2006
2nd printing, 2008
ISBN 978-0-9778123-3-2

It is permissible for teachers, schools and community groups that have adopted this curriculum through Reach for College! to make copies of any part of this book as needed. All others please seek permission.

Reach for College! is a 501(c)(3) nonprofit organization dedicated to promoting equity by increasing and supporting the number of traditionally disadvantaged students who pursue and complete post-secondary education.

The **Reach for College!** curricular materials were developed specially for college access for traditionally disadvantaged students. The materials are being used:
- in advisory periods.
- during school time in classes dedicated just for SAT prep and college access.
- during school time incorporated into already existing classes such as junior or senior English classes.
- in out-of-school time programs.

Acknowledgements and Heartfelt Gratitude

Several individuals and groups lent their expert and experienced ideas to this book. Without their generous help and time, this book would not be as helpful to students as we hope it is. Those individuals are:

C. Don Bradley, Associate Dean of Recruitment Services & Houston Recruitment, Oklahoma University
Dr. Bertha D. Minus, Associate Provost for Student Retention, University of the District of Columbia
Dr. Sandra G. Yates, Chair, Retention Committee
Retention Committee, University of the District of Columbia
Marian Smith, Office of Recruitment and Admission, University of the District of Columbia
William Brahame, Student, University of the District of Columbia

For more information:
www.reachforcollege.org

Reach for College!
700 12th Street, Suite 700
Washington, DC 20005

Email: info@reachforcollege.org

Phone: 202-246-7357

COLLEGE & REAL LIFE SKILLS FOR SUCCESS
AFTER GRADUATION

Table of Contents

INTRODUCTION 1

1. **CONGRATULATIONS! GET READY TO FOCUS ON YOUR NEXT GOAL** 3
   Congratulations, feel proud, focus on the next stage of your life 3
   Don't let typical stumbling blocks keep you from your goal 4
   Remember your reason for going to college and plan to graduate 6

2. **WELCOME TO COLLEGE! GETTING STARTED** 9
   Getting started in college can feel overwhelming, but you can do it! 9
   Placement tests and pre-college classes are early steps along the way to your goals 10
   Some college vocabulary 12
   Signing up for classes—catalog, schedule of classes and registration 19
   You are on your way! 24

3. **MAKE A SUCCESSFUL SOCIAL TRANSITION TO COLLEGE** 25
   Be smart as you go through the transitions ahead 25
   Beware of the social transition 26
   Maintain a successful time balance between your social and academic lives 26
   Be open to new people and different ways of living 29
   Be open to new experiences 30
   Be true to your values and to yourself 30

4. **MAKE A SUCCESSFUL ACADEMIC TRANSITION TO COLLEGE** 33
   Accept the challenge to succeed academically 33
   Study skills that work—Be aware of your learning environment 37
   Study skills that work—Improve your ability to focus 39
   Study skills that work—Be an active learner 41
   Study skills that work—Become an active learner when you read 42
   Study skills that work—Taking notes 45
   Study skills that work—Taking tests 48
   Study skills that work—Studying for mid-terms and final exams 50
   Use what works for you 52
   Adopt an attitude of success for the academic transition 56

5. **MAKE A SUCCESSFUL EMOTIONAL TRANSITION TO COLLEGE** 59
   Be aware of the emotional transition to college and help yourself to success 59
   Homesickness is real but short-lasting 60
   You might feel pulled by family issues at home 61
   You might miss friends you've left behind 62
   You might feel academically unprepared and inadequate at first 63
   You might feel out of place at first 63
   You might wonder about your new identity—Who are you becoming? 65
   Success with the emotional transition helps you become a better, wiser person ... 66

6. **MANAGE YOUR TIME** 69
   Time management in college is crucial to success 69
   Prioritize..71
   Plan 73
   Short-range time management for today..75
   Changing routines adds extra time to your day 76
   Yearly calendar 77
   Weekly calendar..78
   Use good time management techniques and discipline to reach your goals.....................79

7. **MANAGE YOUR INDEPENDENCE AND PERSONAL RESPONSIBILITIES** 81
   Handling personal responsibilities can start you on a solid path toward adulthood.........81
   Your responsibility—Keeping your personal space and clothes clean.............................82
   Your responsibility—Eating well 82
   Your responsibility—Staying healthy..83
   Your responsibility—Your safety...85
   Your responsibility—Managing your money 87
   Making a budget and living within it..87
   Learn about bank accounts—Checking and savings 90
   Vocabulary of banking..92
   Banking forms...93
   Credit cards 99
   Buying a car—Getting a loan 101
   Student loans to finance higher education 107
   Understand the value of keeping a good credit report...108

8. **MANAGE YOUR FINANCIAL AID**...113
   You'll need to manage your financial aid...113
   How do I get financial aid? The FAFSA is the key...115
   Financial aid offices at colleges are crucial—get to know your financial aid adviser 115
   Need more money? 120
   Is it smart to take out a loan to pay for college? 122
   Will I be given the same amount of financial aid automatically every year?..................122
   Obtaining financial aid is a critical part of the process of moving toward your goals 123

9. **CREATE A "SUCCESS NETWORK" FOR YOURSELF** 125
   Your success is your responsibility...125
   Lean on me..126
   Colleges make many resources available to students. Use them!...................................126
   Establish relationships with faculty, administrators and mentors....................................129
   Jump on problems as soon as you notice them. Don't wait..130

10. **TIPS FOR STUDENTS WHO ARE WORKING, COMMUTERS OR PARENTS** 133
    Challenges for students who are working, commuting or parenting 133
    Tips for succeeding at college while you're working, commuting or parenting 134
    Even though it's challenging, don't give up..135

INTRODUCTION

Congratulations! You will soon be graduating from high school. This is a milestone in your life, but as with any milestone, marking how many miles you've come, this shouldn't signify the end of the journey. It's just one point along the way. Yes, certainly, graduation is a time to rejoice. But **high school graduation is *not* the finish line. If you're smart, and we know you are, you'll continue your journey until you graduate from the higher education school that you've set as your goal.**

Hopefully, you have already been planning for the next step in your life journey—further education that will lead you to the career you want and to the success you're aiming for. Planning is important, because as any team will tell you, you have to have a game plan and a strategy in order to win. The more detailed the game plan, the higher likelihood of success; so, **if you haven't already, sit down and strategize with yourself and your parents. What exact steps are you going to take to get to your career goal?**

Then, **you need to anticipate and prepare for what to expect as you move forward.** By getting into the mindset of where you're going, anticipating what might be difficult areas and common pitfalls, you'll be ready for them and can avoid them, or know what to do if you do hit them. It's all about preparation—actual and mental—and that's what this book is about. **This book will help you anticipate what to expect after you graduate from high school and begin the next phase of your education. It will give you valuable tips that will prepare you to be successful once you get there.**

The next steps of your exciting journey are about to begin—anticipate, prepare, and get ready. Real life and real success lie just ahead!

Chapter One

"To achieve your goals, you must be crystal-clear about what you want and why you want it."
~Victoria Johnson, Author

CONGRATULATIONS! GET READY TO FOCUS ON YOUR NEXT GOAL

In this chapter you will:
- Understand that high school graduation (commencement) is not the end; it's really the beginning, commencing the next stage of your life.
- Learn that *focusing* on your goals ahead will help you reach them.
- Know that there are typical stumbling blocks that cause many young adults to lose their focus and not reach their goals
- Become aware that there are some useful mindsets to help you stay focused and get around typical stumbling blocks.

CONGRATULATIONS, FEEL PROUD, FOCUS ON THE NEXT STAGE OF YOUR LIFE

Congratulations on the accomplishment of getting close to finishing high school and moving on to the next phase of your life. It's important to remember that graduation ceremonies are called 'commencements', which means commencing or beginning something. When you walk across that stage at your commencement ceremony, you should be thinking of walking out of high school and into the beginning your new life. **High school is not the end; it's just the beginning.**

If you have been thinking ahead and planning for your future, you probably already have some plans for further education. This education might be in a training or trade program or in college. Either way, you have already done yourself a huge favor, because, as you know, **higher education provides you with a ticket to a better economic future.** See the chart below.

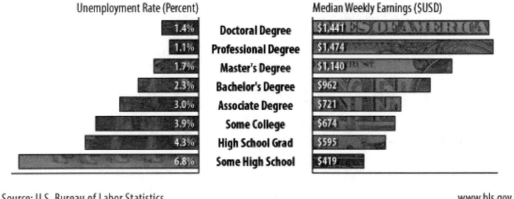

Now, is the time to be preparing to make a successful transition to any type of postsecondary education. **And this book will tell you what to expect and how to succeed in the next phase of your education.**

If there is one overall gigantic tip which can help you succeed in higher education it can be summed up in one word: focus. Focus means to see clearly and to concentrate. It means a mental mindset of determination and everyday efforts to carry through on that mindset. If you can maintain your focus, nothing can keep you from success. Throughout this book, we will be showing you all the big and little ways to help you keep your focus in the upcoming years, so you can reach your goals. So walk proudly, think ahead and begin to focus.

DON'T LET TYPICAL STUMBLING BLOCKS KEEP YOU FROM YOUR GOAL

Make a promise to yourself that you will treasure the feeling you have when you walk across the stage at your high school commencement. And then promise yourself you will savor that same feeling again when you walk across the stage at your college commencement.

From the moment you graduate from high school, you have to begin to focus on graduating from college or the training or trade program you've decided on. This is because **all kinds of people and temptations might try to keep you from attaining your goals.** These people and temptations can come in the form of:

- **A job**—you might wonder why you're going to college when you have a job already or will have one during the summer that pays pretty well.
- **Fear**—you're nice and comfortable in your neighborhood among your friends and family and it's scary to think of going away or even going across the city to tackle something new and challenging.
- **Tired of school**—you're sick of homework, studying, tests, and teachers nagging at you. Why would you want to start that all over again?
- **Your family**—even though they might say they want you to go to college, they are pulling you back home in all sorts of subtle and not-so-subtle ways.

- **Your friends**—girlfriends, boyfriends, or just friends you've known since elementary school are asking why you want to move away from them.

All these people and temptations are very real stumbling blocks. Young adults just like you, fall over them and never reach their goals or get partly there and then give up. That's where the determination and focus has to kick in.

Stumbling blocks	**Thoughts to keep focused on completing higher education**
Job	The job might seem to pay well now, but $5.25 per hour only yields $11,000 per year and $7.25 per hour only yields $15,000 per year. The minimum amount needed for a family of four to live comfortably is $55,000 per year. The typical high school graduate earns $11,000-28,000 per year. The typical college graduate earns $40,000-85,000 per year.
Fear	Venturing out of your comfort zone is usually scary for the first few days of any new experience, but after that it becomes your new routine, and you will have grown into a bigger person in the process.
Tired of school	Of course, when you get to the end of something, you're tired. Tired at the end of a race, tired at the end of a day of work, but that doesn't mean you don't race anymore if you're an athlete or don't go back to work the next day. It just means you take a break, rest, then start up again. Keep in mind that college is different from high school. Teachers don't nag, you have much more freedom in what you study and how you study. There is usually very little, if any, 'homework' that you have to turn in. College is a totally new learning experience.
Your family	Whether they say it out loud or not, your family *wants* you to be successful. Nobody ever raised a child in hopes that he or she would turn out to not do well in life. So, go ahead and make them proud—succeed beyond their wildest dreams and you will be doing the best thing possible to make your family happy. Yes, they might have problems. All families have problems that might distract you and draw you back into issues at home. But you know deep down that the *best* thing you can do is to get your education, so you can have a better economic life for yourself *and* them.
Your friends	Whether you go away to college or live at home and commute, your relationships with your friends, including girlfriends and boyfriends, are likely to change. For one thing, you're going to be making new friends at college and expanding your worldview. This will probably feel difficult and might put a strain on long-time relationships, but if they are *true* friends, they will want the best for you and will risk change.

REMEMBER YOUR REASON FOR GOING TO COLLEGE & PLAN TO GRADUATE

One of the best ways to keep your focus is to remember why you wanted to go on to higher education in the first place. If you keep that in front of you, keep your eyes always on that prize, then it's easier to deal with the people and temptations that might appear in front of you.

Everyone has his or her own reasons for going to college. These reasons should be very specific to you. Your reason for going to college should *not* be, "Because I want to be successful." That's not specific enough and will not be enough to carry you through rough patches you might encounter. **You need to visualize for yourself very specifically what you want to be doing five or ten years from now.** How do you see yourself? What setting will you be in? What will you be doing? What will you be wearing? What types of people will be around you? What will you be accomplishing? How much money will you be earning? What kind of car will you be driving?

As you visualize these large and small things, remember we're not talking about the same fantasy game you dreamed up when you were 11-years-old, in which you were a princess or a sports hero. If you're still stuck there, you need to update your image, and do your research. You want to be a sports trainer? How much does a trainer make? What kind of education is required? How many years? What certifications or licenses are needed? How do you get hired? What kind of network do you need to establish to move up in that world?

Think about your future and specifically plan for it. Set up a plan for achieving your goals and then refer to this plan whenever you need to in order to keep focused.

Assignment #1:

My Reason for Going to College & My Plan for Achieving My Goals

Note: College students *can and do* change their ideas of what they want to study (major in) every single day. Many times they change their career goals as they learn more about the subject area and realize that they're interested in something different. That is okay. Nobody will ever force you to stick with something you're not going to enjoy.

The point of this assignment is to acknowledge that studies have shown you are much more likely to succeed if you go into your postsecondary education with a solid goal in mind. That is the best way to assure yourself the follow-through necessary to achieve whatever goal it is that you finally choose!

1. **I *appreciate* and *respect* myself for continuing my education. I intend to complete my educational program and graduate!**
My main reason for going to college is: _____
     (Be specific! To say you want to be successful in life is not enough.)

2. My second reason for going to college is: _____
(This might be something such as to help your family, to improve your community, or to defy the statistics, etc.)

Reach for College!

...after Graduation _____ **7**

3. I understand that to reach my goal I need to get educated and/or trained in the following way:
   (Circle one)

   Apprenticeship in a trade   Associate's Degree program (2-year college)

   Bachelor's Degree (4-year college)   Bachelor's Degree + graduate school

4. I expect that this educational path to my career will take about _____.
   (How long?)

5. There is an exam, license, certificate, or degree I must pass and obtain.
   ☐ Yes   ☐ No

The name of this exam, license or degree is called _____.

6. I understand that once I complete my education and obtain the necessary license, certificate or degree and get a job, that I will earn about _____ per year.

7. To me the best thing about accomplishing this goal will be _____
_____

Create a timeline plan to reach your goals.

What will you be doing toward your goals, and the lifestyle you want in the following years?

1st year after high school_____

2nd year after high school_____

3rd year after high school_____

4th year after high school_____

5th year after high school_____

6th year after high school_____

7th year after high school_____

8th year after high school_____

"The tragedy in life doesn't lie in not reaching your goal.   The tragedy lies in having no goal to reach."
~Benjamin E. Mays

Reach for College!

Chapter Two

"Education is our passport to the future, for tomorrow belongs to those who prepare for it today."
~Malcolm X

WELCOME TO COLLEGE! GETTING STARTED

In this chapter you will:
- Understand that there are a lot of things to do to get started in college, as with anything new, but you can do it.
- Learn that placement tests help the college get you started in the right classes.
- Begin to learn and use some of the vocabulary relating to people, places and things on college campuses.
- Practice using college catalogs and class schedules in preparation for registering for classes.

GETTING STARTED IN COLLEGE CAN FEEL OVERWHELMING, BUT YOU CAN DO IT!

There is so much to do to get started in college. You might be feeling it already if you've been accepted to a college, and they are deluging you with packets of information and paperwork. There are so many decisions to make, forms to fill out, and all kinds of unfamiliar things to complete and return, that it might begin to feel like one big hassle and that it's not worth it. Stifle that feeling!

Remember that getting started in *any* new thing is a hassle—whether it's a new job, a new house and neighborhood, or a new school. Remember that there is a lot to do at first, but everything calms down eventually, and you adjust to your new place and your new routine. Getting everything set for college is no different.

These are some of the usual things you'll probably have to do to get started in college.
- Make sure all your paperwork is in for:
    1. Immunizations (shot record)
    2. Financial aid
    3. Proof of residency (if going to a public college)
    4. Health insurance

5. Dorm information (if you're living on campus)
6. Meal plan information (if eating on campus)
7. Final high school transcript

- Move all the stuff you're bringing to college into a very small room that you will share with a complete stranger.

- Take placement tests in reading, English and math.

- Find and meet with your advisor to decide on a class schedule and get his/her signature on the appropriate paperwork.

- Spend time in the financial aid office getting all the details of your financial aid package worked out.

- Register for classes—learn how the registration process works and survive it.

- Endure the crush in the bookstore to buy books after getting over the shock of seeing how much they cost.

- Attend various orientation functions and get a lot of information dumped on you, so you will feel like you'll never understand it all.

- Survive the whirlwind of meeting a whole lot of new people who work at the college and try to figure out how they're going to impact your world.

- Try to remember the names and faces of all the new students you meet and present yourself as a likeable and cool individual they would like to get to know.

This list is not meant to overwhelm or discourage you, it's meant to prepare you, so you're not shocked or worried that something is not right when everything comes at you at once, and when you feel befuddled and overwhelmed. Remember that *everyone* goes through these same things when they're going on to higher education. It's new, strange and bewildering to them too.

Just realize it's going to be a tough and exciting first couple of weeks, and then strap on your seat belt for the ride. Remember your accomplishments:
- You did all the work and graduated from high school!
- You prepared for and took the SAT!
- You completed all the applications and got into college!

You are a smart and resourceful individual. You can take on and meet this challenge too.

PLACEMENT TESTS AND PRE-COLLEGE CLASSES ARE EARLY STEPS ALONG THE WAY TO YOUR GOALS

Placement tests are one of the many things you must complete in order to start college. Since high schools across the country are all different in what they require of their students, the way colleges determine if you have learned all the high school material and are ready for college-

level work is by giving you a placement test. Every college requires them unless you have demonstrated your academic proficiency by getting a high score on the SAT or on AP exams.

Many times, the placement tests indicate that you have to take some basic pre-college classes before you start actual college-level work. You will know you are taking the pre-college classes because they are numbered before the 100 level. College level classes are generally numbered as 100 level classes for first-year students (such as English 101), 200 level classes for sophomores, 300 and 400 level classes for juniors and seniors.

Please do not be discouraged by the placement tests or by the fact that you might be required to take pre-college classes before you can begin regular college classes. About 40% of students entering college now must take these classes. It is a harsh reality that your elementary, middle and high school years might not have prepared you adequately to do college-level work. It's not your fault, but it is important that you now have a realistic understanding of where you stand.

There is often a huge disconnect between what is required of you in high school and what is required of you in college. The college doesn't want to throw you into classes that you are not prepared for and in which you might fail. So, they have you take pre-college classes to bring your skills up to college level. That is okay. Think of how you learn songs in church. You sing the same songs over and over until you master them before you move on to the next song. The pre-college classes will be the same way. Some of the information will look somewhat familiar because you probably had a bit of it in high school. But now the class will help you master it and move up to the next level, onto the next song.

You should definitely strive to do well on the placement tests and even review for them. Take them seriously. Do NOT blow them off as unimportant! If you can do well on them, then you will not have to take the pre-college classes. This will save you time and money. On the other hand, if the placement tests indicate that you have to take the pre-college classes, then step up and get started. Keep in mind that you are not alone, and this is simply one more step on your way to your goals. By the way, studies show that even though you might come into college slightly behind, you will catch up and do just fine.

Assignment #2:

Practice with college placement test questions.

Look at a sample of questions that are likely to be on college placement tests. You can practice with sample questions from the Montgomery College "Accuplacer" test at:
www.montgomerycollege.edu/Departments/AssessCtr/AccuplacerSamplePF.html
It would be a good idea to see if you can answer them because your college will probably have a similar test. Then if you see that you might need to review some concepts, plan to do that over the summer, so you'll be ready to take the placement tests at your school.

SOME COLLEGE VOCABULARY

As with anything new—a new job, new streets in a new neighborhood, new classes—there are new words to learn. College has many specialized words that might seem confusing at first, but will soon be second nature to you. To speed up your learning process and help you feel more confident during your first few days, here is a list of common terms you're likely to hear and their meanings.

People

In high school you have been familiar with the faculty and staff and have known them as your principal or headmaster, assistant principals, counselors, teachers, registrar, coaches, etc. People play similar roles in a hierarchy at college; they just have different titles.

President and Vice Presidents
The President of the college is the overall head or chief executive of the school. Then there are one or more Vice Presidents. Each Vice President is usually in charge of a certain section of the university, such as the Vice President for Health Professions, Vice President for Student Affairs, etc.

Provost
The Provost is usually the chief academic officer of the college, which means that he/she is in charge of everything having to do with classes and teaching. In some colleges the Provost is called the "Academic Dean."

Deans
There are usually several Deans at a college, each in charge of a particular aspect of college life. For instance, there is usually a Dean of Students, who is in charge of anything having to do with concerns of students. This might range from parking issues to fairness issues. There might also be a Dean of Housing, a Dean of Summer School, a Dean of Honors Programs, a Dean of Admissions. Some colleges also name the head of various "schools" within the college a Dean; so, there would be a Dean of Arts and Sciences, a Dean of Engineering, etc.

Registrar
The Registrar is the person in charge of "registering" students for classes and keeping track of grades and the classes the students have completed. Usually the registrar's office issues an online or paper "Schedule of Classes" that will be available each semester. From this schedule, you can decide which classes to sign up for.

Bursar
The Bursar is the person you pay for the classes you take and for your room and board, if you live on campus. Usually, signing up for classes is a multi-step process. You talk to your adviser (see the next entry below) to choose your classes. The adviser signs off on them. You go to the registrar's office to register/sign up for the classes. Then you go to the bursar's office to pay for them.

Advisers
Usually you will be assigned an adviser at the beginning of your first year. This person, who is an instructor or professor at the college, is supposed to help you choose classes that will head you in the right direction toward your degree and career goal. Your adviser can also be a person you can turn to if you need help or advice.

RA's (Resident Assistants)

Resident Assistants are older students who live in the dorms and are paid by the college (usually by getting free room and board) to handle problems of students in that dorm. You can go to your RA with issues about your room, bathrooms, or with more personal issues and they will try to help.

Full Professor

This is the highest rank among the "teachers." It is based usually on scholarship (research they've done and published), academic recognition, sometimes on years in the university, and tenure. (Being a tenured professor means the person can stay at that school until retirement if they choose.)

Associate Professor

Next in rank after professor, this person is usually tenured and is involved in research in his or her field.

Assistant Professor

Next in rank after Associate Professor, but this person may be in the early part of her or his career. He or she may be tenured or not and working on research and publishing.

Instructor

This is the beginning rank. Sometimes instructors are part-time employees.

TA—Teaching Assistant

This is sometimes a graduate student who is assisting a professor, or they may be assigned to their own course, sometimes for teaching experience.

Adjunct Professor

This is usually a professor from an adjacent institution who is hired to teach part-time.

The hierarchy of rank above does not indicate how you should address someone. If they have a Ph.D., you should call them Dr. _____. But, when in doubt about whether to address someone as "Dr." or "Mr." or "Mrs.," it is certainly acceptable to address your college teacher as "Professor."

Most college teachers have multiple responsibilities, including advising students, attending to administrative duties, developing curriculum, supervising academic programs, doing research and writing of their own. Sometimes they have limited time to talk with you, but most truly want to be helpful, especially to diligent students.

If you'd like to talk with any professor, check his/her office hours and visit them during that time or make an appointment. Many professors like to build relationships with students. This helps them get to know you better. And it helps *you* in the long run not only with the class, but also by making it easier to ask for recommendations and advice. Building relationships with professors helps you to create a "success network." (See Chapter Nine—Create a "Success Network" for Yourself—for more on this.)

Places

At your high school, most likely everything is contained in a single building, and all the offices, classrooms, athletic facilities, etc. are part of that single building and the grounds right around it. Generally, colleges are bigger and have multiple buildings. Very often each building is devoted to one aspect of college life. For example, there is a separate building for the offices that run the college, a separate building or buildings where students reside, a separate building or buildings for classrooms.

You will learn your way around campus and learn the names of buildings quickly. Every college or university is different, so you'll need to learn the particulars of your school. But there are some buildings that are constant at almost every school. These are listed below.

Administration Building
There is always a building devoted to the administration of the college. This is often where the President, Vice President and Provost's Offices are located. Usually, the Registrar's office and Financial Aid offices are also located there.

Dining Hall or Student Union
You need someplace to eat and hang out. This is the dining hall or Student Union. Frequently this building will also house the bookstore and recreational rooms that might have such things as TV's and arcade games.

Athletic Facilities/Gym
Most campuses have athletic facilities that are available for any student to use. These might have weight rooms, aerobic workout machines, pools, basketball courts, tracks, etc.

Classroom Buildings
Classrooms are often grouped together in one particular building devoted to related subject matter. For example, there might be a Chemistry or Sciences Building, a Nursing Building, a Computer Sciences Building, etc.

Library or Libraries
Most campuses have more than one library. Usually there is one large general library that is centrally located on the campus. Then there are often smaller libraries, sometimes in other buildings, that are for students studying in certain majors, such as a Law Library, a Business Library, etc.

Dorms
At large colleges there are many dorm buildings. Some schools put all the first-year students in a particular dorm. Other schools let students choose which dorm they want to live in. On all campuses there are certain dorms that students prefer over others, based on how close they are to dining halls, on how new they are, etc. These are all the little idiosyncrasies you will learn once you get there.

Centers

Often there are "Centers" on college campuses that provide very helpful services to students and might be housed in any of a number of buildings. **It is to your great advantage to find these centers on your campus and use them.** Examples of these are:

- **Career or Placement Center**—Every school has an office or series of offices where students can go to look up information on various careers and jobs. Career center staff is there to help you in making decisions about a career and in guiding you toward getting good jobs in that career. Often career centers have listings of job openings.

- **Health Center**—Sick? Go to the health center. Usually part of the fees you pay to the college in your "tuition and fees package" is student health insurance, so you can go to the health center for free and they will take care of you. Whether you are suffering from a bad cold and need cough medicine, sprained your ankle playing touch football, or feeling depressed, the health center is there for you.

- **Tutoring Center**—Having trouble in a class? Nearly all schools have a tutoring center with staff or students available many hours of the day to help you with any subject area. This is a great resource and you shouldn't be shy about using it to the fullest.

- **Counseling Center**—College can be a stressful place, especially during those crazy first few weeks when you're making the adjustment to college life, being away from home, on your own, and studying a lot. If you are feeling upset, stressed, sad, angry or any other thing and want to talk to someone and get some helpful advice, then go to the Counseling Center. (This might be part of the Health Center.) Like at all the other Centers, help is waiting, and you just have to walk in the door.

Building names

Most colleges name their buildings after people who gave money to the school, past presidents, famous graduates, etc. So, you'll find that students and professors will refer to places on campus as "Peabody Hall" or "Jones Center," for example. At first this will be confusing and you will wonder why they don't just say, "the library" or "the administration building." But as you get used to associating the name with the place, it won't seem so strange to you anymore.

Categories, types of classes, majors, degrees

In high school, everyone is pretty much from the same neighborhood, takes the same kinds of classes, and is on the same type of schedule heading toward graduation. In college this is not true. There are many different types of students, from many different places, all studying different things, on different timetables. Here is some of the vocabulary to get you prepared for what you'll find when you get there.

Course/course numbering system

In college, "classes" are called "courses," as in, "Are you taking the Women's Studies *course* on diaries?" And all courses are numbered. Generally, the numbering system goes like this:

10-99	Pre-college level courses
100-199	Courses for first-year college students
200-299	Courses for second-year students
300-499	Courses for third- and fourth-year students

Reach for College!

500-800   Courses for students who have graduated from college, also known as Graduate students

For instance, if you see that a class is numbered 101, you will know that this is an introductory-level class. If a class is 301, you will know that it is an advanced level course. Usually you are not allowed to take higher-level classes until you have completed and passed the introductory level classes.

Prerequisites—Often in the schedule of classes that the registrar puts out every term, course descriptions will end with a notation such as, Preq: 110, 112. That means it is pre-required (prerequisite) that you have taken and passed course numbers 110 and 112 before you can sign up for the course listed.

Credits/credit hours—Each course in college is assigned a certain number of credits or credit hours. Most often, a class carries 3 or 4 credit hours. This usually means that you attend this class that many hours per week. The number of credits is important because you have to accumulate a particular number of credit hours in order to graduate. This number varies from college to college, but usually it is in the range of 120-135. So, if you take 16 credit hours per semester—a full "load"—you would graduate in 4 years. (16 credit hours x 8 semesters = 128 hours.) The number of credits each course carries is listed in the college catalog as part of the description of courses and in the schedule of classes the registrar issues each semester.

Lecture/seminar—College courses have a variety of formats. Some are "lecture" classes, which means that the professor stands up in front of the class, which is usually a large class, and lectures for most, if not all, of the class session. The students take notes, read the textbook, take a mid-term and a final exam, and that is the course. A "seminar" on the other hand is usually a small class that sits around a table to discuss and share ideas. Course work consists of intensive reading and writing outside of class. During your time in college, you will probably have both types of classes.

Major/declare a major—Your "major" is what you decide is your focus of study. Usually there are set majors at colleges. In other words, you will choose one that is already laid out. (You can't, for instance, decide that you want to study the history of cartoons on TV. There probably is no major such as that.) There are hundreds of majors to choose from, but, as you know, not all schools have all the majors. You have to choose your college partly based on what you want to study.

Usually in your sophomore year you "declare a major." This means that you sign some paperwork, which says that you are aiming toward a particular major. This enables the college to guide you toward successfully completing this program of study. In order to complete a major, there are a set number of courses you have to take in that area of focus. Often it is around 45 credit hours you have to complete in your major in order to graduate. This is part of the total number of hours needed to graduate, not in addition to it.

Minor/declare a minor—Most students also have a "minor." This is their secondary area of focus. Usually it is related to their major. So, for instance, a student might be majoring in computer networking and minoring in business administration so he/she could be a network

...after Graduation

administrator for a company or business after graduation. Often around 25 credit hours are required for a minor. Usually a student declares a minor at the same time he/she declares a major. Again, this is just part of the total number of hours to graduate.

Pre-professional degrees—There are some majors that are specifically designed to lead toward further education. These are pre-professional programs, such as pre-law, pre-med, pre-dentistry. Usually there are very specific requirements to get into pre-professional majors, so it's a good idea to check on that either before or as soon as you get to college.

Study abroad/semester abroad programs—Colleges offer programs in which you can continue working toward your degree (your diploma from college) by studying elsewhere. It is a popular option to "study abroad." You can do one semester or one whole year in a college or university in another country. This is a mind-expanding experience because you learn so much about the other country and about yourself in addition to what you learn from the books. Most colleges have study abroad options that make it easy to sign up to study out of the country for a while, and amazingly, it often doesn't cost any more than your usual fees.

Undergraduate—"Undergraduate" students are students in college from freshman year through senior year. An "undergraduate" program is one that applies to those years.

Graduate—"Graduate" students are students who have graduated from college and are now studying for a higher degree, such as a Master's, a Ph.D., or a professional degree, such as an MD.

Colleges and schools—Universities often subdivide the areas of study into different "Colleges and Schools." So, there is likely to be a "College of Arts and Sciences," a "School of Education," a "College of Dentistry," etc.

Departments—Within the Colleges and Schools a further subdivision is departments. (In smaller colleges, instead of calling the different areas of study colleges or schools, they are called Departments.) There would be an African Studies Department, a Health Education Department, or a Science Department, etc.

Academic calendar—The "academic calendar" is the school's calendar from the first semester in the fall through the summer sessions in the following summer. It lists all important dates, such as registration times, when classes begin and end, final exam periods, etc. It's important to have a copy of your college's academic calendar and keep an eye on important dates as the year progresses.

Assignment #3:

Practice using college vocabulary.

1. What is the title of the overall head of the college or university? _____

Reach for College!

2. What is the title of the person in charge of everything having to do with classes and teaching? _____

3. Who do you usually talk to about which classes to sign up for, who will guide you to choose classes that will lead toward you career choice? (Hint: This person usually has to sign a form listing the classes you will take before you can register for the classes.) _____

4. Whose office registers students for classes and keeps track of the classes students have taken and their grades? _____

5. What does a TA do? _____

6. If you don't know if you should address your teacher as Dr., Mr., or Mrs. what is an acceptable way to address any college teacher? _____

7. You move into your dorm room but find that you can't get the Internet to work, who do you talk to about that? _____

8. List three buildings that are usually found on college campuses and their functions:
   Building   Function
   _____   _____

   _____   _____

   _____   _____

9. If you are interested in getting a job to gain experience in your career field during your college years or employment after you graduate, where on campus should you go to get help with this?
_____

10. You need usually 120-135 "credits" or "credit hours" to earn a college degree. Usually how many credits do you earn per class you take and pass? _____

11. What is an "undergraduate"? _____

12. What is a "study abroad" program? _____
_____

Would you like to participate in a study abroad program when you get to college? _____

If so, what country would you most like to go to? _____

13. What is the "academic calendar?" _____

...after Graduation 19

14. Why will your college's "academic calendar" be important to you? _____

___

SIGNING UP FOR CLASSES--
CATALOG, SCHEDULE OF CLASSES AND REGISTRATION

One of the main things you will need to do when you get to college is to sign up for the first classes you'll take. In most cases you will have some classes that every first-year student is required to take, such as a Composition/Writing class, a math class and maybe some kind of freshman orientation seminar. But then you will be able to choose other classes you'd like to take. (You will probably take three or four classes altogether per semester.) Typical other freshman classes are in psychology, history, science, language, art, or music. Unlike high school, there are a *lot* of classes to choose from. So how do you figure out what to take?

This is where your adviser comes in. As mentioned, you will be assigned an adviser, who is a member of the faculty, and can advise you about good classes to take toward your career goal and can help you with any other questions or problems you might have. But **if you want to do some research about classes before you see your adviser, the college "catalog" is the place to start.**

Catalog

Every college has a "catalog". This is a very useful little book (and most are online now too) because it tells you about everything you would want to know about the college, classes, student life, campus resources, etc. The catalog will tell you, for example, what majors the school offers and the exact classes and numbers of classes you need to take in order to graduate with a degree in that major. The catalog will also give you a description of *each* of those classes. This is important information to have to help you make informed decisions about what classes you'd like to take.

The following is a page from a typical college catalog describing classes in the Communications Department. Look at the type of information provided:
- The abbreviation for the department is "COMM" and refers to the Communications Department.
- The course numbers, such as 100, 340, etc. (Remember that generally the 100-level classes are for first-year students, the 200 level classes for second-year students and so on.)
- The prerequisites required. (Classes that should be taken before this one.)
- A description of what will be covered in the class.

Are there any classes there that look interesting to you?

CMSC 477 Optimization (3) Prerequisites: (AMSC/CMSC/MAPL460, AMSC/CMSC/MAPL466, or AMSC/CMSC/MAPL467) with a grade of C or better and permission of department; or CMSC graduate students. Also offered as AMSC477. Credit will be granted for only one of the following: AMSC477, CMSC477 or MAPL477. Linear programming including the simplex algorithm and dual linear programs; convex sets and elements of convex programming; combinatorial optimization, integer programming.

CMSC 498 Selected Topics in Computer Science (1-3) Prerequisite: permission of department. An individualized course designed to allow a student or students to pursue a selected topic not taught as a part of the regular course offerings under the supervision of a Computer Science faculty member. In addition, courses dealing with topics of special interest and/or new emerging areas of computer science will be offered with this number. Selected topics courses will be structured very much like a regular course with homework, project and exams. Credit according to work completed

CMSC 499 Independent Undergraduate Research (1-3) Prerequisite: permission of department; restricted to Computer Science and Computer Engineering Majors. Students are provided with an opportunity to participate in a computer science research project under the guidance of a faculty advisor. Format varies. Students and supervising faculty member will agree to a research plan which must be approved by the department. As part of each research plan, students should produce a final paper delineating their contribution to the field.

COMM – Communication

COMM 100 Foundations of Oral Communication (3) Not open to students who have completed COMM107. Credit will be granted for only one of the following: COMM100 or COMM107. Prerequisite for advanced communication courses. A study of oral communication principles, including verbal and nonverbal language, listening, group dynamics, and public speaking. Emphasis in this course is upon the application of these principles to contemporary problems and upon the preparation of different types of oral discourse.

COMM 107 Oral Communication: Principles and Practices (3) Not open to students who have completed COMM100. Credit will be granted for only one of the following: COMM100 or COMM107. A study of and practice in oral communication, including principles of interviewing, group discussion, listening, informative briefings, and persuasive speeches.

COMM 125 Introduction to Interpersonal Communication (3) Concepts of interpersonal communication including perception, language and meaning, nonverbal communication, listening and feedback.

COMM 170 Foundations of Listening (3) Role, process, and levels of listening behavior and the development of listening skills.

COMM 200 Critical Thinking and Speaking (3) Theory and practice of persuasive discourse analysis and composition. Research techniques, logical and rhetorical conceptions of argument, and technical principles for persuading in public venues.

COMM 220 Small Group Discussion (3) Principles, methods and types of interaction occurring in small groups with an emphasis on group discussion and decision-making.

COMM 230 Argumentation and Debate (3) A study of the fundamental principles of reasoning, analysis, and evidence preparation of debate briefs and presentation of standard academic debate.

COMM 231 News Writing and Reporting for Public Relations (3) Two hours of lecture and two hours of laboratory per week. Prerequisite: Grammar competency demonstrated by a score of 52 or higher on the TWSE and permission of department. Limited to COMM majors. Credit will be granted for only one of the following: JOUR201, JOUR201P, JOUR231, or COMM231. Formerly JOUR 231. Introduction to writing and researching news and information media for public relations; laboratory in newsgathering tools and writing techniques for public relations.

COMM 232 News Editing for Public Relations (3) Two hours of lecture and two hours of laboratory per week. Prerequisite: Grade of C or better in COMM231 or equivalent and permission of department. Limited to COMM majors. Credit will be granted for only one of the following: JOUR202, JOUR202P, JOUR232, or COMM232. Formerly JOUR 232. Copy editing, graphic principles and processes, news and information technologies for public relations.

COMM 250 Introduction to Communication Inquiry (3) An introduction to the field of communication. Definitions, models, and contexts of communication; rhetorical theory and rhetorical criticism of discourse.

COMM 288 Communication Internship (1-6) Prerequisite: permission of department. Repeatable to 6 credits if content differs. An individual experience arranged by the student with the instructor. Does not satisfy communication major requirements. 45 hours of supervised internship per credit hour with communication professional. Not a substitute for COMM386.

COMM 298 Selected Topics in Communication (3) Repeatable to 6 credits if content differs. Special topical study of contemporary issues in communication.

COMM 324 Communication and Gender (3) The creation of images of male and female, and masculine and feminine, through communication, the differences in male and female communication behaviors and styles, and the implications of those images and styles for male-female transactions.

COMM 330 Argumentation and Public Policy (3) Contemporary theories of argumentation with special emphasis on methods of formulating and critiquing public policy argument.

COMM 340 Communicating the Narrative (3) The role of narratives in communicating messages and development of strategies to effectively communicate the narrative form through storytelling, oral reading, and anecdotes.

COMM 350 Public Relations Theory (3) Prerequisite: Grade C or better in JOUR201, JOUR231, COMM231 or COMM250; or permission of department. For COMM majors only. Not open to students who have completed JOUR330. Credit will be granted for only one of the following: COMM350 or COMM430 or JOUR330 or JOUR530. Formerly JOUR 330. The historical development and contemporary status of public relations in business, government, associations and other organizations. Application of communication theory and social science methods to the research, planning, communication and evaluation aspects of the public relations process.

COMM 351 Public Relations Techniques (3) Prerequisite: A grade C or better in JOUR202, JOUR232 or COMM232; and COMM350. For COMM majors only. Not open to students who have completed JOUR331. Credit will be granted for only one of the following: COMM351 or JOUR331. Formerly JOUR 331. The techniques of public relations, including news releases, publications and printed materials, audio-visual techniques, speeches and special events. Application of these techniques in laboratory and field projects.

COMM 352 Specialized Writing in Public Relations (3) Prerequisite: A grade of C or better in COMM351. For COMM majors only. Not open to students who have completed JOUR332. Credit will be granted for only one of the following: COMM352 or JOUR332. Formerly JOUR 332. Public Relations writing for science, technology, health, medicine, corporate finance, educational policy, law and government in broadcast and technical media, as well as newspapers, magazines, proposals, speeches and correspondence.

COMM 354 Public Relations Programs (3) Prerequisite: COMM350. Not open to students who have completed JOUR334. Credit will be granted for only one of the following: COMM354 or JOUR334. Formerly JOUR 334. Analysis of eight major programs typically carried out by public relations professionals: employee relations, media relations, financial relations, member relations, governmental relations, community relations, fundraising and dealing with activist public.

COMM 360 The Rhetoric of Black America (3) An historical-critical survey of the rhetoric of Black Americans from the colonial period to the present.

COMM 370 Mediated Communication (3) Prerequisite: COMM250. Junior standing. Analysis and critique of structure, performance, content, effects, and future of mediated communication.

COMM 383 Urban Communication (3) A study of communication variations in the urban setting with emphasis on communication problems encountered in ethnic relations. Strategies for improving communication.

COMM 386 Experiential Learning (3-6) 45 hours of supervised internship per credit hour Only 3 credits may be used to fulfill the requirements for the Communication major. Prerequisite: permission of department. Junior standing. For COMM majors only. Supervised internship experience with communication professionals. Relation of academic training to professional experience.

COMM 388 Communication Practicum (1-3) Prerequisite: permission of department. Repeatable to 3 credits if content differs. Supervised professional-level practice in communication.

COMM 398 Selected Topics in Communication (3) Repeatable to 6 credits if content differs. Topical study of contemporary issues in communication.

COMM 399 Honors Thesis (3) Nine hours of laboratory per week. Prerequisite: permission of department. For COMM majors only. Repeatable to 6 credits if content differs.

COMM 400 Research Methods in Communication (3) Prerequisite: COMM250 and an introductory course in statistics. For COMM majors only. Philosophy of scientific method; role of theory; research ethics; empirical research methods (measurement, sampling, design, analysis).

COMM 401 Interpreting Strategic Discourse (3) Prerequisite: COMM250. For COMM majors only. Principles and approaches for practical analysis of discourse designed to shape audience opinion.

COMM 402 Communication Theory and Process (3) Prerequisite: COMM250. For COMM majors only. Philosophical and conceptual analysis of communication theories.

COMM 420 Theories of Group Discussion (3) Current theory, research and techniques regarding small group process, group dynamics, leadership and decision-making.

COMM 421 Communicating Leadership (3) Not open to students who have completed COMM498L. Examines the nature of leadership, theories of leadership from a communication perspective, relationships between leadership, authority, power, and ethics. Explores leadership responsibilities, commitments, and actions.

COMM 422 Communication Management (3) Communication policies, plans, channels, and practices in the management of the communication function in organizations.

COMM 423 Communication Processes in Conferences (3) Group participation in conferences, methods of problem solving, semantic aspects of language, and the function of conferences in business, industry and government settings.

COMM 424 Communication in Complex Organizations (3) Structure and function of communication within organizations: organizational climate and culture, information flow, networks and role relationships.

COMM 425 Negotiation and Conflict Management (3) Role of communication in shaping negotiation and conflict processes and outcomes.

COMM 426 Conflict Management (3) Recommended: COMM425, COMM250, and COMM402. Role of communication in managing conflict processes.

COMM 430 Public Relations Theory and Techniques (3) Prerequisite: JOUR201 or equivalent; and permission of department. Not open to students who have completed COMM350. Credit will be granted for only one of the following: COMM350, COMM430, COMM630, JOUR530 and JOUR630. Formerly JOUR 530. Theories relevant to the strategic management of public relations and techniques used in programs to communicate with publics of organizations

COMM 435 Theories of Interpersonal Communication (3) Prerequisite: COMM400 or permission of department. Major theoretical approaches and research trends in the study of interpersonal communication.

COMM 450 Ancient and Medieval Rhetorical Theory (3) Prerequisite: COMM250. For COMM majors only. Credit will be granted for only one of the following: COMM450, or COMM650. A survey of rhetorical theory in the ancient and medieval periods. Emphasis is placed on the theoretical problems that gave rise to its development within both periods. Authors include Isocrates, Plato, Aristotle, Cicero, Quintilian, Hermogenes, Martianus Capella, Aurelius Augustine, Alberic of Monte Cassino, Geoffrey of Vinsauf and Robert of Basevorn.

COMM 451 Renaissance & Modern Rhetoric Theory (3) A survey of rhetorical theory in the renaissance and modern periods. Emphasis is placed on the theoretical trends that dominate rhetorical thinking during both periods—especially in Great Britain. Authors include Wilson, Sherry, Rainolde, Day, Hyperius, Cox, Ramus, Talon, Bacon, Pascal, Fenelon, Sheridan, Campbell, Blair, and Whately.

COMM 453 The Power of Discourse in American Life (3) The potential of language forms and strategic discourse to create, perpetuate, and alter patterns of political and cultural behavior. The influence of contemporary political and cultural discourse on public understanding, public policy, and day-to-day life.

COMM 455 Speechwriting (3) The study of message strategies in order to research and develop effective speech texts appropriate to speakers and their audiences in various public contexts.

COMM 458 Seminar in Political Communication (3) Prerequisite: COMM250. Repeatable to 6 credits if content differs. The examination of special topics for and theories of political communication.

Reach for College!

Schedule of Classes

Remember that the registrar puts out a "Schedule of Classes." Since not every class listed in the catalog is offered every semester, the schedule of classes tells you which classes are being offered that semester, what time they are offered, and who's teaching them. Usually the Class Schedule is online too. Here is the schedule for some of the Communications classes offered for a particular semester. Notice all the information provided:

- The abbreviation for the Communications Department = COMM
- The course number—COMM 125, COMM 200
- The Title of the course
- The number of credits for successful completion of the course
- The method of grading—Regular or Pass/Fail
- Brief description of the course
- Who may take the course
- The numbers 0101, 0201 refer to the fact that several of these same classes are being offered. You choose which time and which teacher you want to take. (However, in most cases in this particular class schedule, the teacher has not yet been decided on, so only Staff is listed.)
- Days and Times the class is given.
- Location of the class (listed below as SKN or ARM or CHM, etc.)
- How many students will be in the class (Seats)
- What books are required

COMM107S Oral Communication: Principles and Practices; (3 credits) Grade Method: REG/P-F.
Not open to students who have completed COMM100. Credit will be granted for only one of the following: COMM100 or COMM107.
```
1901(15622) STAFF (Seats=24, Open=24, Waitlist=0) Books
     MWF...... 2:00pm- 2:50pm (SKN 0104)
```
COMM125 Introduction to Interpersonal Communication; (3 credits) Grade Method: REG/P-F/AUD.
Concepts of interpersonal communication including perception, language and meaning, nonverbal communication, listening and feedback. This course is restricted to students of the former College of Human Ecology, College of Business and Management, College of Education, College of Journalism, College of Letters and Sciences, and students with the following major codes: 0108F, 01020, 01030, 01021, 01031, 1506A, 12230, 12120, 12130, 21030, 1307D and 00001.
```
0101(15632) STAFF (Seats=24, Open=24, Waitlist=0) Books
     TuTh......11:00am-12:15pm (ARM 0118)
0201(15633) STAFF (Seats=24, Open=24, Waitlist=0) Books
     TuTh......12:30pm- 1:45pm (ARM 0118)
```
COMM200 Critical Thinking and Speaking; (3 credits) Grade Method: REG/P-F/AUD. CORE Humanities (HO) Course.
Theory and practice of persuasive discourse analysis and composition. Research techniques, logical and rhetorical conceptions of argument, and technical principles for persuading in public venues.
```
0101(15643) STAFF (Seats=2, Open=2, Waitlist=0) Books
     TuTh......12:30pm- 1:45pm (CHM 1224)
0201(15644) STAFF (Seats=2, Open=2, Waitlist=0) Books
     TuTh...... 2:00pm- 3:15pm (CHM 1224)
0301(15645) STAFF (Seats=2, Open=2, Waitlist=0) Books
     MWF.......11:00am-11:50am (PLS 1115)
0401(15646) STAFF (Seats=2, Open=2, Waitlist=0) Books
     MWF.......10:00am-10:50am (PLS 1115)
```
COMM230 Argumentation and Debate; (3 credits) Grade Method: REG/P-F/AUD.
A study of the fundamental principles of reasoning, analysis, and evidence preparation of debate briefs and presentation of standard academic debate.

Reach for College!

```
0101(15667) STAFF (Seats=24, Open=24, Waitlist=0) Books
       TuTh...... 8:00am- 9:15am (PLS 1164)
0201(15668) STAFF (Seats=24, Open=24, Waitlist=0) Books
       TuTh......12:30pm- 1:45pm (PLS 1113)
0301(15669) STAFF (Seats=24, Open=24, Waitlist=0) Books
       TuTh......11:00am-12:15pm (PLS 1113)
0401(15670) STAFF (Seats=24, Open=24, Waitlist=0) Books
       TuTh...... 9:30am-10:45am (PLS 1164)
```

COMM231 *(PermReq)* **News Writing and Reporting for Public Relations; (3 credits)** Grade Method: REG/P-F/AUD.
Prerequisite: Grammar competency demonstrated by a score of 52 or higher on the TWSE and permission of department. Limited to COMM majors. Credit will be granted for only one of the following: JOUR201, JOUR201P, JOUR231, or COMM231. Formerly JOUR 231. Introduction to writing and researching news and information media for public relations; laboratory in news-gathering tools and writing techniques for public relations.

```
0101(15680) Toth, R. (Seats=18, Open=18, Waitlist=0) Books
       M.........12:00pm- 1:50pm (EGR 3140)
       W.........12:00pm- 1:50pm (EGR 3140) Lab
```

COMM232 *(PermReq)* **News Editing for Public Relations; (3 credits)** Grade Method: REG/P-F/AUD.
Prerequisite: Grade of C or better in COMM231 or equivalent and permission of department. Limited to COMM majors. Credit will be granted for only one of the following: JOUR202, JOUR202P, JOUR232, or COMM232. Formerly JOUR 232. Copy editing, graphic principles and processes, news and information technologies for public relations.

```
0101(15691) Toth, R. (Seats=18, Open=18, Waitlist=0) Books
       Tu........ 1:00pm- 2:50pm (EGR 3140)
       Th........ 1:00pm- 2:50pm (EGR 3140) Lab
0201(15692) Toth, R. (Seats=18, Open=18, Waitlist=0) Books
       Tu........ 3:00pm- 4:50pm (EGR 3140)
       Th........ 3:00pm- 4:50pm (EGR 3140) Lab
```

You create your own schedule of classes you want to take

So, putting together the catalog and the schedule of classes for each semester, you can then figure out *what classes* you want to take, *what teacher* you want and *when* you want to take the class. As you can see this offers you a lot more freedom than high school!

A typical freshman schedule might look like this:

M, W, F	10:00-11:15	English 101
M, W, F	2:00-3:15	Math 101
T, Th	1:00-2:50	Computer Science 100
T, Th	3:00-4:50	Psychology 101
M	1:00-1:50	Freshman Seminar

Obviously, your classes are not on the structured high school 8:30 AM-3:30 PM schedule. You have a lot more time in your days, and each day is a little bit different.

Registering for classes

After you've done some research on one or two classes you'd like to take (in addition to what will be *required* that you take in freshman year,) and you've seen your adviser and devised a good schedule using the schedule of classes, then you are ready to register. Each school has its own registration procedures and many are online now, so learn about how to register and then take the time (and have the patience) to go through the process. Understand that, as in the first

Reach for College!

time with anything, you are bound to run into a problem or two and it might be a bit frustrating until you get the hang of it. This is just the way it is. Soon you'll be a pro at this process, but there is a first time for everything, and you've just got to get through this learning process. Don't forget—you can *always* ask for help!

Add/Drop Classes

Here is something to remember: there is another big advantage in having freedom to take what you want in college, and that is that if you don't like a class or a particular professor or feel you cannot yet be successful in a class, you can get out of the class by "dropping it." Within a certain time period, usually a couple of weeks after classes start, you can drop one class and add another one to substitute for it without any penalty. You just have to do the proper paperwork through the registrar's office. However, **it is *extremely* important to *actually do* the paperwork to drop a class. If you decide you don't like a class you must *not* simply stop going to it or else you will fail it, that failure will be added to your transcript and your GPA, *and* you will still have to pay for the class.**

Assignment #4:

Practice using a catalog and a class schedule.

1. Practice fitting a class into your schedule, so you have no conflicts, by looking at the class schedule above. Pretend you want to take COMM 200—Critical Thinking & Speaking. You already have classes on MWF at 9:00-9:50 and 11:00-11:50 and on T, TH at 12:30-1:45. Do you have room in your schedule to fit in the COMM 200? _____ If so, at what time? _____

2. Go online to the website of a college you hope to attend. Search the catalog for several classes you would like to take. List those here:

_____

_____

_____

_____

_____

3. Now look at the Class Schedule for this semester and see if you can find those classes. Not all of them might be offered this semester. If one or two are offered, write down the days and times they are offered, and if available, write down the name of the professor, and the location of the class on campus.

Class number	Name of class	Days & times	Name of Prof.	Location
_____	_____	_____	_____	_____
_____	_____	_____	_____	_____
_____	_____	_____	_____	_____
_____	_____	_____	_____	_____

4. After you've registered for a class and started going to it, you find that the class is not going to work for you for some reason. What can you do?

_____

What must you be *absolutely* sure to do in this situation?

_____

YOU ARE ON YOUR WAY!

As you can probably tell it takes a lot of momentum to get everything started in college, but once this initial administrative work is done, then the simple routine, day-to-day life of college rolls along. You are on your way!

"It takes steady nerves and being a fighter to stay out there."
~Wilma Rudolph

Chapter Three

"It is far easier to engage in too much or too little of anything than to hit that special place called moderation."
~Johnnetta B. Cole

MAKE A SUCCESSFUL SOCIAL TRANSITION TO COLLEGE

In this chapter you will:
- Understand that you will be making several important "transitions" in the first several months of college.
- Learn that to be successful in making the social and academic transitions you will need to spend more time on academics than on socializing.
- See that there will be many opportunities to stretch and expand into new areas of interest and to learn about many different types of people.
- Understand that the ideal way to successfully navigate the social transition is to maintain a balance of trying new things but also to remember and live by your core values.

BE SMART AS YOU GO THROUGH THE TRANSITIONS AHEAD

As you move out of high school and into the next phase of your life, you should recognize that you will be making several important transitions. These transitions are moving you gradually to a new place in your life. They are helping you to grow and become a bigger, more mature person. Some of these transitions are:
- To officially enter the world of adulthood, at age eighteen—with greater independence and greater responsibilities.
- To move out of the restricted life of high school and into the freer world of higher education.
- To adjust to the changes in your new world at college or in a training program.

The more aware you are of these transitions and the challenges they sometimes pose, the smarter you can be about navigating them successfully.

BEWARE OF THE SOCIAL TRANSITION

One of the biggest challenges students face in going to college is successfully making the social transition. This might seem as if this would be the easiest transition to make. After all, how hard can it be to hang out with new friends or stay up late playing games or partying? All of a sudden you have a lot of extra time that you used to have to spend at school and now you have a schedule where you might only have to be in class a couple of hours a day. And, in fact, most professors do not take attendance, so you don't really have to be in class every day. What is so challenging about all this?

Well, unless you can learn to balance your time and keep the social life in perspective from the first day of college, you can be in academic trouble within two weeks. And remember that the reason you're in college is, actually, for the academics.

Now no one is saying that you should hide yourself in your room or in the library and not speak to a soul until the end of each semester. The social side of college and the friendships you build there are also very important, but you have to remember your focus. The focus of your life in college is to graduate! You can't have that wonderful feeling of success walking across the stage and into the admiring arms of your family and friends, unless you do the work to get there.

MAINTAIN A SUCCESSFUL TIME BALANCE BETWEEN YOUR SOCIAL & ACADEMIC LIVES

How many hours a day should you study in college?

So much about being successful in college has to do with time-management. This is especially true in making the social transition. You must keep in mind that once you go to college, you have much more freedom in how you choose to spend your time than you've ever had before. In high school, the time in your day is probably spent something like this:

High School Daily Schedule

- In school & transit to school   7 hours   7:00-3:00
- Sports or after-school job   2-4 hours   3:00-7:00
- Homework   2-3 hours   7:00-10:00
- Meals   1-2 hours   Scattered through day
- Sleep   <u>6-8 hours</u>   10:00-6:00
                                  17-24 hours

This daily schedule has left you little or no free time for long periods of your life, since you pretty much had no options except to do these things at these times.

But when you go to college, your daily required schedule is likely to look something like this:

College Daily Schedule

- In class   1-4 hours   Any time from 7:00 AM-10:00 PM

All the rest, you *choose* to do. In fact, you even choose at what times you have your classes. For example, you could *choose* to set up your class schedule so that you only go to classes Mondays, Wednesdays, and Fridays and you have no classes at all on Tuesdays and Thursdays.

You *choose* when to eat and when to sleep. You *choose* what time to come home to your room; there is no curfew. You *choose* whether or not to do the reading for your class. (And there usually is no 'homework' to hand in.) You *choose* whether or not to participate in sports or to have a job. In other words, your time is *completely* your own to spend how you want to spend it. And that is the trap that many students fall into with the social transition!

With all this freedom and no one watching you, no one demanding anything of you, it's easiest, and most fun, to spend it playing, and that's what a lot of students do. They talk with their new friends until 4:00 in the morning. They play dominoes, cards, and videos games. They party every night. They spend two hours eating and talking at every meal. They get very involved in some campus activity and spend days working at it. **And when they turn around, they are failing their classes**.

This is not meant to be a scare tactic, it's meant to prepare you. Get ready to meet this temptation head-on. The easiest way to make sure you don't fail the social transition (which automatically leads to a failure in the academic transition) is to balance your time. How can you effectively do this? You balance your time by being aware of this challenge.

Here is a rule of thumb that will serve you very well. Generally, if you are taking a course for three credits that means you will be in that class for three hours per week. **Want to know how many hours per week you should be devoting outside of class to be successful in the course? Double the class hours. Three hours of class = six hours of reading and studying per week for that class.** Now, you still have a great deal of freedom because you can study those six hours any time you want during the week. If you're a night owl, you could do the reading and studying for the class from 2:00 AM- 4:00 AM three nights per week, and then sleep until noon if you have no morning classes the next days. But you should plan to spend six full hours preparing for the class.

How much time per week does this mean altogether for a full load of classes? If you're taking 12 credit hours, then you should be in class for 12 hours per week and reading/studying for 24 hours per week. Given that there are 168 hours in a week, this still gives you a lot of free time. So, let's see how this might play out on a daily basis.

12 Credit Hours—An example of a daily schedule

Monday	4 hours in class, 3 hours studying
Tuesday	No class, 5 hours studying
Wednesday	4 hours in class, 3 hours studying
Thursday	No class, 5 hours studying
Friday	4 hours in class, 0 hours studying
Saturday	No class, 2 hours studying
Sunday	No class, 6 hours studying
Total	**12 hours in class, 24 hours studying**

Of course, as we've said, you can study any time you want. You could, for example, to choose not to study on the weekends at all. But that would mean that you would not spend as much time during the week socializing. It's all up to you. But **the crucial thing to remember**

Reach for College!

is to double the amount of class time as a minimum for study time if you are to make a good social transition and academic transition.

How many hours a day should you socialize in college?

Let's look at the time-balance in the social transition another way. Here's another rule of thumb: If the time you spend on social interaction supersedes the time you spend on academics, then you will not make an adequate social or academic transition.

When you get to college keep mental track (or even on paper) of the number of hours you spend socializing. This should include:
- Time eating with friends
- Time talking with friends in dorms, in libraries, in student gathering places
- Time playing games
- Time at parties, athletic, or night events
- Time spent on campus involvement activities such as clubs, service, etc.
- Time on dates
- Time on phone or e-mail

Then keep track of the number of hours you are in class and the number of hours you (honestly) spend reading and studying.

If your social interaction time is greater than your time spent on academics, then by the time you realize it, you might be already failing. Your social time is valuable to your growth and to your mental state. There is no question about that, but there has to be a balance and moderation. **If your social lives and academic lives are in proper balance, then you will survive and thrive at college and make a successful social transition.**

Assignment #5:

How do your social and academic lives balance now?

1. Practice keeping track of the time you spend socializing and the time you spend in class and studying now. Write down a close estimate of your times below.

Activity	Hours spent per day	Hours spent per week
Academic Life		
In school	_____	_____
Doing homework/reading/studying	_____	_____
Totals	_____	_____
Social Life		
On phone or e-mail or texting	_____	_____
Socializing after school	_____	_____
Socializing in evenings	_____	_____
Socializing on weekends	_____	_____
Totals	_____	_____

2. Are your academic and social times in balance now? ☐ Yes ☐ No

3. Are you satisfied with your grades now? _____

4. Keeping in mind that college will be academically more challenging than high school, will you change anything about this balance when you go to college? ☐ Yes ☐ No

If yes, how and what will you change? _____

_____

BE OPEN TO NEW PEOPLE AND DIFFERENT WAYS OF LIVING

One of the best aspects of socializing in college is that you are exposed to a rich variety of new kinds of people who often have different backgrounds from your own. If you've had the typical high school experience that means you've been going to school with kids from your neighborhood or nearby surrounding area for many years. Chances are, you all come from similar backgrounds and neighborhood cultures and share many things in common.

But college is often a big mixing bowl. You'll meet people from other parts of the country and other parts of the world. They'll likely have different slang, different popular clothing styles, different home backgrounds, and cultures that might all be new to you. Get ready to be surprised and interested. Be open to learning about these fellow students because many times you can learn as much from your fellow classmates as from your professors. You might end up adopting some of their talk, some of their style, and some of their points of view. And they will probably be just as interested in learning about your background and might adopt some of what you bring to the interaction too. It's all part of the social transition to the college experience.

You can help this process along by adopting an attitude of genuine friendliness, non-judgmental tolerance, and openness that will help make you known as a good person to talk to. Since **all the first-year students are new at the same time and all are usually coming into the situation, like you, not knowing anybody or maybe only knowing a couple of people, everyone is eager to get to know each other.** There are no cliques or groups yet, no already-established groups of friends. This is a rare opportunity to start fresh since no one knows you. You can put your best foot forward, wear your friendliest smile, and put your heart into a lot of new and wonderful friendships.

It is true that very often the friendships you make in college are ones that last your whole lifetime. So be open, be tolerant, be friendly, put your best self out there and your new friendships will be off to a good start.

BE OPEN TO NEW EXPERIENCES

College is also a great time to try out new experiences. Usually there are many student-run clubs and groups that are eager for and welcome new members. **Stretch out of your comfort zone by trying something completely new and different** such as:

Hiking	Playing the steel drums
Scuba diving	Debating
Painting	Participating in a service project that moves you
Canoeing	A hundred other things that might be going on

Not only will you learn new things that might become lifelong interests, but you'll have fun, and connect with new people you might enjoy.

Try out being a leader too. **There are also many opportunities in college to take on leadership roles.** The student governing body is only one of many ways you can get involved as a leader. All of the many clubs and groups always need help and appreciate when people step up to help run things. You'll find that in college students run many more things than in high school, so, look for your niche and get involved. This will build your self-confidence and give you great experience that you can put on your resume for jobs later on.

Assignment #6:

What new activities or groups might you want to participate in at college?

1. Go to the website for the college you're most interested in attending and look under "Student Activities" or some other tab along those lines. Find the list of student groups or clubs available at your potential school. List five or six that you think you might like to find out more about and/or participate in?

_____   _____

_____   _____

_____   _____

2. What leadership role might you enjoy at your new school?

_____   _____

BE TRUE TO YOUR VALUES AND TO YOURSELF

All the time you're trying out new things, getting to know new people and venturing into new experiences also remember to be true to yourself and what you value. Like the balancing

act between your social and your academic lives, it's also a balancing act to expand out and try new things but at the same time not go too far beyond what you feel is right for you and what you treasure. **Remember and live by your core values.**

Too often, with all the new freedom and independence students feel being on their own for the first time, they go wild. They stay up to all hours; they imitate fellow students who seem to be so cool by doing crazy, reckless things; they let down their guard about drinking, drugs and sex. Not only can this experimenting lead to failure in school, but it can also lead to problems that can't be undone, such as accidents in which people are hurt or killed and pregnancies.

Again, this is not meant to be a scare tactic. It's meant to honestly tell you, from the experience of many students, the pitfalls that some students succumb to in trying to make the social transition. Yes, it's good to feel independent, adult, and in control of your own life and your own decisions to do what you want. But, **it's also good to feel responsible and confident enough of yourself to make the right choices for you.**

An example of this is an issue that confronts many students at college: drinking or drug use. On most college campuses parties are greased with alcohol consumption and/or drug use. Sure, this might loosen everyone up, but too often students drink or drug to excess. (Especially on majority white campuses excessive drinking is often the rule. It is how they socialize.) Quite often this leads to problems—people doing stupid things which cause accidents, getting sick and vomiting, and alcohol poisoning which sends kids to the emergency room. Excessive alcohol use can also lead to anger and belligerence, friends turning against friends, and unwanted sexual encounters that can cause disease or pregnancy.

So you need to make a conscious decision, a thought-through, adult decision about what you care about and what you value in these types of situations. **Are you going to follow the crowd or are you going to 'play the tape to the end' and see where this might lead? Think about and sort through what's important to you and then promise yourself to live by that.**

In the situation of excessive drinking, for example, if you have decided beforehand that you don't want to drink at all or very much, then when you get to the party—go for the soda. Yes, you might get teased at first, but if you have a glass in your hand after awhile people aren't going to keep checking what is in it. They are going to be much more concerned about what's in *their* glasses instead. As they get stupider as the night goes on, you can be grateful that you're not saying dumb things or throwing up like they are. And you can respect yourself in the morning and get to your studying while they're nursing their hangovers of nausea and an aching head.

Assignment #7:

What core values do you want to live by at college?

1. Think about and write down at least five things you value about yourself and how you conduct yourself that you want to remember to live by at college. An example of this might be

"I always try my best in every situation." Or, "I always try to be a gentleman." Or, "I think ahead to consequences and always try to make good choices."

_____
_____
_____
_____
_____

2. There might be things you want to change about yourself, and moving on to college is a perfect time to do this. Write down at least three new attitudes or ways of acting that you might like to try at college. An example of this might be, "I wish I was more outgoing. I'll try to be friendlier and more outgoing."

_____
_____
_____

"In anything I do, I want to be the best."
~Will Smith

Reach for College!

Chapter Four

> *"No matter how you feel. No matter how you think the professor feels about you. It's important to have a consistent presence in the classroom. If nothing else, the professor will know you care enough and are serious enough to be there."*
> ~Nikki Giovanni, Poet, Professor of English

MAKE A SUCCESSFUL ACADEMIC TRANSITION TO COLLEGE

In this chapter you will:
- Understand that you will have to rise to the challenge of college-level work.
- Learn what daily things you can do to succeed academically.
- Practice study skills that work:
  1. Be curious, adopt an attitude of wanting to learn.
  2. Create a good learning environment.
  3. See how to become an active learner in your reading, note taking, and test taking.
  4. Practice ways to get the most out of your reading through the SQ3R method.
  5. Practice active note taking with the Cornell method.
  6. Practice some new test-taking tips.
- Adopt an attitude of success.
- Know that determination and hard work will pay off in the end.

ACCEPT THE CHALLENGE TO SUCCEED ACADEMICALLY

Let's be very honest about several things:
- If you are accepted into college, then you are definitely smart enough to go. No question.
- College work is a step up from the work you've been doing in high school, so it will probably be more challenging at first.
- Your schooling up to this point might not have adequately prepared you, which means you might have some catching up to do. But you *will* catch up.

So, knowing that you're smart and will probably face some academic challenges at first, what can you do to succeed? That is what this chapter is about.

First you have to accept the challenge that you *want* to succeed academically and you will do what it takes to make it and graduate. Second, there are several things you can do to help yourself succeed academically starting on day one when you arrive on campus. If you do these things consistently, you will succeed, without doubt. Here they are.

Take the Placement Tests seriously.

You only have to take the Placement Tests once, as you enter college, right before you register for your first classes. But they are *not* simply one more formality of starting school. They determine *where* you will start in your course work. If you just breeze through them or sleep through them without really trying, you might do poorly and be placed in pre-college level classes that might seem too easy once you're in the class. Further, these pre-college classes gain you *no* college credit toward graduation, and yet you *do* have to pay for them. So, it will literally save you time and money if you can do well enough on the Placement Tests to start directly with college level classes. Take the Placement Tests seriously. Practice placement test questions. (See Assignment #2 in this book for practice questions.) Review for the tests.

Go to class *every* day and sit up front.

Since professors rarely take attendance formally in college classes, it is tempting to skip classes or to slump in the back and snooze. However, this is an extremely bad idea. Even though professors might not call the roll, they do notice who is there and who is paying attention if the class is small enough. That way they know who is taking their class seriously and who isn't. Guess which student they're more likely to want to help in office hours when things get tough.

But most importantly, you *learn* things in class. Hopefully, you will read the assigned reading beforehand, so you know generally what the class is going to be about before you arrive. But being in class gives you the huge advantage of then learning what is most important about what you've read. And this isn't just knowledge you can use on the test (although that's important information to have too,) what you learn in class is likely what you'll need to know about this subject in *life*. The professor emphasizes in lectures or in discussion what is important, stimulates your thinking about the subject, and gives you key things to remember. This is called teaching and learning and that is what you're paying for in college. So don't waste money by not going to class.

Do the assigned reading on time.

There is nothing worse than going to a class when you have not done the required reading. Then have to sit through hearing the professor drone on about something and you have no idea what she/he is talking about or have no idea of what everyone is discussing. Not only do you get very little value from the class, but you might even get confused because you don't know the basics of what's being talked about. It's so much better to inform yourself by doing the reading before you come to class. Then you will understand what's going on, will get your questions answered, and can be an active participant.

Take notes and ask question in class.

Be active in class. You will learn more if you're busy—busy thinking, busy taking notes, busy asking questions. Remember that the more modes of getting information into your brain— through the actions of reading, listening, writing, and talking—will all contribute to your brain processing the information and holding onto it. So get active and stay active in all your classes.

Hand in assignments on time.

What could be more obvious? Want a good grade? Do the work. Turn it in at the required time. In college there is no busy work. The professors don't need you to be handing in a lot of work they have to grade. They just want you to turn in a couple of things to show to them that you understand what they're teaching. So usually, the only assignments required are a paper or two. That, along with a couple of tests, usually add up to your grade. Get the work done and hand it in. Simple.

Study in advance for exams, not just the night before.

Just as there are generally very few assignments in college classes, there are also generally very few tests. Most often there is just a mid-term and a final exam. Of course, this means a lot more of your grade is resting on those two tests, and they each cover a lot of material. So, unlike in high school, where you might be able to cram for a weekly test the night before, that won't work in college. It pays to start reviewing and studying a week or more before these tests.

Talk to your professor.

Your professor *wants* you to succeed. Your professor *likes* to talk to interested students. Remember that they wouldn't have taken, as their life work, to teach young adults unless they liked interacting with young adults. So, if you're having a problem in the class, or even if you're not, go talk to your professor. Brief comments after class are good. Go visit during office hours, or, make an appointment. All are good times to talk. Your professor is more likely to read your papers and essays more appreciatively if she/he knows you a little and knows where you're coming from.

Talk to other students in your classes.

Sometimes the best way to learn things and help them stick is to learn them with a study group of fellow students. If you feel this would be helpful in some of your classes, then ask a couple of fellow students if they'd like to form a group and work together to seriously tackle the subject matter.

Use campus resources.

Every college *wants* you to succeed. They *want* you to get a lot out of your classes and graduate. They also realize that some courses are harder than others and that everybody needs help sometime. So, all colleges provide resources to help students personally and academically. You just need to learn where they are and tap into them. Usually there are writing and math labs, tutors available for most subjects, and other special resources that are free and waiting. You just have to take the initiative to track them down and to go there often. They can help a lot.

Focus and persevere.

Your greatest asset to help you academically will have to come from within you. If you are determined and if you are focused, then you will succeed. If you persevere when things get tough, if you ask for help and take all the steps above, then you will succeed. Your own inner strength and determination will have to be the strongest factor, because if you want it badly enough, you will find a way through the obstacles to your goal. So make a promise to yourself and visualize your future. Then go out and work your hardest to reach that future.

STUDY SKILLS THAT WORK

Once you have made a decision to do all of the things listed above—go to all your classes, do all the reading and assignments on time, ask for help, etc.—there still remains the nitty-gritty of actually doing the reading and learning in each class. What is the best way to succeed at that on a daily basis? The answer lies in boosting your study skills. **The next few sections will give you very specific suggestions of how to succeed academically with reading, studying, taking notes, etc.**

'Study skills' is probably a term you've heard thrown around for years. And chances are you know lots of little mind games that you use to help you remember and spit things back for tests. You know fast ways to answer questions at the end of chapters for homework. You've figured out how to do the minimum and still please your teachers. But in college, these things probably won't get you by anymore. You are going to have to read more, remember more, and write more than you've ever had to do before. This is not said to scare you, but to prepare you. You need to begin practicing a new set of study skills that will help you to be as successful a student as you can be.

STUDY SKILLS THAT WORK—GET CURIOUS

First, your attitude toward each of your classes makes all the difference. You've noticed it yourself. **When you are interested in and curious about something, the learning is easier and the grades are better.** Right? **So, the first step toward becoming a great student is to adopt an attitude of curiosity in *all* of your classes.**

Make an effort to see why some kids in your English class really get into the reading. Don't just skim through the reading or avoid it altogether as you might have been doing, but take time and concentrate on it, think ahead to what the discussion might be about and what you might be able to add. Formulate questions about the reading, things you don't understand, that you can ask in class. Other people might have the same questions.

In other words, get curious about what's in those books. Tell yourself that you *want* to learn about them. And this new attitude will carry you far. Things might just begin to seem more interesting, and there is a very good chance that you'll do well in those classes.

Assignment #8:

What is your attitude toward learning? Are you curious?

Answer the questions below very honestly.

1. What is your favorite class? _____ Are you interested, eager to learn, and curious about what goes on in that class? ☐ Yes ☐ No Do you find it's easy to learn in there? ☐ Yes ☐ No Do you get good grades in this class? ☐ Yes ☐ No

2. What is your least favorite class? _____ Are you interested, eager to learn, and curious about what goes on in that class? ☐ Yes ☐ No   Do you find it's easy to learn in there? ☐ Yes ☐ No   Do you get good grades in this class? ☐ Yes ☐ No

3. Do you think that if all of your classes were as interesting as your favorite class, then you'd enjoy all your classes and learn better in all of them? ☐ Yes ☐ No

4. Do you think it might be possible for you to adopt an attitude of trying to get curious about things in all of your classes? ☐ Yes ☐ No

5. Do you think this might help your grades in your least favorite classes? ☐ Yes ☐ No

If you've answered yes to #4 and #5 above, then make a commitment to yourself below to try out this attitude change starting now:

6. I am willing to make a commitment to try to get curious about my least favorite class as an experiment to see if it gets easier for me and to see if my grades improve.
☐ Yes ☐ No

7. I am willing to make a commitment to do the hard work that might be necessary as if I really *want* to learn something (and not just get through something) in this class.
☐ Yes ☐ No

8. I am willing to take the time to ask for help in order to really understand something in this class and grasp its importance.
☐ Yes ☐ No

9. If I fail at something in this class even after I have put in some hard work, I will not be discouraged, will try to learn from my mistakes, will pick myself up and work harder next time.
☐ Yes ☐ No

10. I will *try* to sustain this attitude of curiosity and *want*ing to learn in this class until the end of the school year.   ☐ Yes ☐ No

---

STUDY SKILLS THAT WORK—BE AWARE OF YOUR LEARNING ENVIRONMENT

Create a learning environment for maximum success. Studies have shown that it is really difficult to pay attention to something that requires concentration, if any of the following are true:

Internal distractions—you are:
- hungry
- tired
- angry
- worried

External distractions—if:
- music is playing
- the TV is on
- someone is talking
- room is too hot or too cold
- you are frequently interrupted

In college many of these **external distractions** are going to be found in your dorm room or in the student cafeteria or sometimes even in the library. The most important thing is that you have to be aware that you cannot concentrate and learn under these conditions. You must find a quiet place where no one will bother you that is comfortable, but not too comfortable so that you won't get sleepy.

Reach for College!

You have to have enough respect for yourself to figure out a way to create as much of an ideal learning environment as you can, because **the more of that good learning environment you can create, the faster and more efficiently you'll learn and remember.**

"Okay", you say, "I can find a quiet place to study, but what do I do about those **internal distractions**, such as hunger, tiredness, anger or being worried about something else?"

First get to know yourself and your rhythms. You've heard the expressions, "Oh, he's a night owl", or, "She's an early bird." Figure out which one you are. You probably already know whether you just can't think in the morning, but you're jazzed and ready to go at night, or vice versa. Work with that.

If you know everyday when you get home from school, you are starving and then after you eat, you get sleepy, don't fight it. Don't think of trying to study then, even if you have a ton to do. You won't get much done. Instead, eat, take a short nap, and get up refreshed and ready to work. If you know you just can't think right after class because your mind is dead, use that time to call friends and relax. Later, after the break, you will be more ready to study. **Tell your friends to call you at 4:00 instead of at 8:00.**

But what if something big is going on--you and your girlfriend are breaking up, your grandmother is very sick, your father lost his job--and you are worried and can't think about anything else? This is the hardest kind of internal distraction. There are some strategies to try, and you might have to use several of them at once.

- Talk to someone about it. Sometimes airing your feelings helps to get them off your mind.

- Talk to several people about it. If you need advice or support, maybe you'll feel better after calling a few people.

- Spend some time alone and figure out what you can and should do right away about the situation. If there is something you can do--go visit your grandmother in the hospital--then do that. If there is nothing you can really do--you listened to your father be angry about losing his job, but ultimately, he's the one who's got to do something about getting a new one—then let it go and do your own work.
- Write down your feelings. Make a list of things you need to do.

- Talk to your professors. Let them know you've got something going on in your life that is affecting your work. They might modify an assignment for you or give you extra time.

Assignment #9:

Evaluate your learning environment.

Think of a challenging class you are currently taking. Pretend your teacher gives you an assignment to be completed tonight: 15 pages to read at the start of a new chapter. Describe how you will do this assignment.

Where will you do it? _____

...after Graduation

Is this where you usually do your homework? _____

What time will you do it? _____

Will you be hungry while you are doing it? _____ Will you be tired? _____

Are you likely to be distracted by thinking about something that might be bothering you while you do it? _____

Will the TV or music be on while you are reading? _____

Are you likely to be interrupted at some point while you're reading? _____

How long, do you estimate, it will take you? _____

What grades have you been getting in that class? _____

Would you like to improve your grades in that class? _____

After having read the information above this assignment about the best kind of learning environment, what suggestions do you have for yourself to create a better learning environment?

_____

_____

STUDY SKILLS THAT WORK—IMPROVE YOUR ABILITY TO FOCUS

Answer the questions below honestly.

1. Does it seem as if almost every time you sit down to read, your mind goes wandering off somewhere else? And when you come back to reality, your eyes have progressed down the page but your mind hasn't.
    Yes _____   No _____   Sometimes _____

2. Do you find yourself half asleep in class sometimes, not sure what the teacher is talking about and no notes on your paper even though the blackboard is covered with writing?
    Yes _____   No _____   Sometimes _____

3. Do things show up on tests that you've never heard of, and so the best you can do is guess?
    Yes _____   No _____   Sometimes _____

4. When you get a test back, if the grade is not one you like, do you stuff the test in your backpack and forget about it?
    Yes _____   No _____   Sometimes _____

Reach for College!

Everyone in the world has had the experience of their mind wandering while reading or sitting in class, supposedly listening. Human beings have the ability to do several things at once. That is why your eyes can be reading right down the page while your mind is dreaming about a delicious ice cream sundae. Your hands can even be writing down what the teacher says in class, while you are mentally planning what you'll be wearing on your date tonight. Often, being able to do more than one thing at a time is useful.

But **as a skilled student, you need to train yourself to focus.** The more completely you focus, the better you will understand the material in the book or in the class that your teacher is presenting and the better you will do on the tests that will come.

How can you learn to focus better? The same way athletes learn to run faster. Athletes analyze their running styles, notice where improvements can be made, and then train to make those improvements. It takes practice. And then more practice.

So, let's analyze your present reading style. Try this experiment. Read the following passage. But as you are reading, every time you notice that your mind has wandered off, make a mark (/) on a scrap of paper.

Finding Out About Student Aid

The Student Guide tells you about federal student financial assistance (SFA) programs and how to apply for them. Approximately two-thirds of all student financial aid comes from federal programs administered by the U. S. Department of Education.

Education or training after high school costs more than ever. But postsecondary education is more important than ever, so you need to learn about as many sources of aid as you can. Sources you can use to find out about federal and other student aid are described below:

- The financial aid administrator at each school in which you're interested can tell you what aid programs are available there and how much the total cost of attendance will be.
- The state higher education agency in your home state can give you information about state aid—including aid from the Leveraging Educational Assistance Partnership (LEAP) Program, which is funded jointly by individual states and the U. S. Department of Education.
- The federal government's Access America for Students web site provides access to a multitude of government resources to assist students in planning and paying for their education. Access America for Students is a federal initiative designed to make interacting with the government easier for students. In addition to providing financial aid information, students can use the web site to file their taxes, search for a job, and take advantage of a host of other government services. The Internet address is: students.gov
- Your public library is an excellent source of information on state and private sources of aid.
- Many companies, as well as labor unions, have programs to help pay the cost of postsecondary education for employees, members, or the children.
- Check foundations, religious organizations, fraternities or sororities, and town or city clubs, including community organizations and civic groups.
- Don't' overlook aid from organizations connected with your field of interest.
- The U. S. Armed Forces also offer financial aid opportunities. For example, all branches of the Armed Forces offer the Reserve Officer Training Corps (ROTC) program, which is a federal merit-based scholarship program that will pay for your tuition, fees, and books, and provide you with a monthly allowance.

- If you (or your spouse) are a veteran or the dependent of a veteran, veterans' educational benefits may be available. Check with your local Department of Veterans Affairs office.

(Source: www.ed.gov/prog_info/SFA/StudentGuide/2000-1)

How many marks did you make on that piece of paper? So your mind wandered off 3, 6, or 10 times. That is similar to your starting time, if you were an athlete in training. That is the time you have to beat in order to improve.

How do you improve? You have to become aware of when you lose focus and tug yourself back to the task at hand. When you are reading or sitting in class and you notice that your mind has wandered off, say to yourself, "That's interesting, now come back here," and gently pull yourself back. Your mind is going to be like a curious dog wanting to sniff at other interesting things on a walk, and your job, as the master, is to tug it back to stay on the path.

This is much easier to do if there are fewer distractions on the path. That is why you turn off the music and ask your friend not to call until later. That is why you sit up straight in class, keep your eyes on the teacher, and have your pen ready. Always be aware of your degree of focus. Soon, the more your mind becomes used to this training, the longer it will be able to pay attention and not wander away so easily.

STUDY SKILLS THAT WORK—BE AN ACTIVE LEARNER

The very best way to improve your ability to focus is to be an active learner. No, that doesn't mean jogging around a track with a book in hand or jumping up and down in class. **Being an active learner means that you are curious about what you are learning and actively want to know more.** You *want* to learn. Remember?

And learning means that you are always making connections—connections between what you already know and the new material in front of you. To make those connections, **you have to be thinking, remembering, and mentally questioning, while you are reading, taking notes, and even while you are taking tests.** You need to be an active learner all the time.

"Whew!" you might say. "This sounds exhausting and hard!" And you know what? It *is* exhausting and hard at first. Ask athletes or musicians if they could do what they are doing now perfectly the first time they did it. Ask them if they got winded and tired at first. Ask them if they got frustrated at times and thought, "This is too hard!" Chances are they will tell you that they felt all those things at first, but they knew the pay off would be worth the hard work and the sweat, so they kept at it.

The gift you've been given is that you are smart. Are you willing to work to get smarter, to improve your skill as a learner—to become a *great* learner, a grade A student? It's going to take effort, practice, and learning a new way of doing things. Are you up for the challenge? How good is your attitude?

Reach for College!

STUDY SKILLS THAT WORK—BECOME AN ACTIVE LEARNER WHEN YOU READ

The SQ3R method has been shown over and over again to be highly effective in getting students interested in their own learning and in helping them be successful. It stands for:

Survey
Question
Read
Recite
Review

If you use this method when you read your assignments, you will be more focused, and therefore be more successful. You will be an active learner.

Survey

Let's say you have been assigned to read a chapter in your book. **The first task, before you even start to read, is to survey the whole chapter. In other words, you look over the pages and preview them, sort of like you look at the preview of a movie.** You see the highlights so you will have an idea of what the story is going to be about in the chapter.

How can you tell what the highlights are? Every textbook author gives you big, fat clues in the form of:
- chapter titles and subtitles
- subheadings within the chapter
- words in bold print
- italicized words
- assignments
- questions at the end of chapters
- things written in boxes
- graphs, charts, maps, and illustrations

You survey the reading by looking at all these things to get an overview of what you are about to read, to see how it is organized, and to get a glimpse of where you are going. This will only take a few minutes, but it will actually save you time as you read because it will be easier to stay focused if you know where things are leading. Your mind will wander less often, and you will begin to see how you might connect old things you know to the new things you are about to learn.

Try this experiment. Please read this short paragraph:

"With hocked gems financing him, he defied all scornful laughter that tried to prevent his scheme. 'Your eyes deceive,' they said. 'It is like a table, not an egg.' Now three sturdy sisters sought truth. As they forged along, sometimes through calm vastness, yet more often over turbulent peaks and valleys, their days became weeks as many doubters spread fearful rumors about the edge. At last, from nowhere winged creatures appeared, signifying the journey's end."

(From *Becoming a Master Student* by Dave Ellis, Houghton Mifflin, Boston, 1997, p. 105.)

You might have trouble knowing what is even going on in this paragraph, let alone trying to summarize it, unless you know a key piece of information first. If you had been assigned to read this and had previewed the assignment and knew that it was about Christopher Columbus, then the whole thing would have made more sense. Re-read it again, thinking about Columbus, about his idea that the world was round not flat as a table, about the three sturdy boats that carried him over calm and stormy seas until land was signified by the birds he saw flying toward him. Then it makes sense.

Similarly, too many students plunge into a reading assignment without ever knowing what's it is going to be about. It's as if they are blind and feeling their way through the chapter, bumping into things and being annoyed at things that pop up and they don't know how they all fit together. It is far better to take a few minutes to *survey* a chapter first to be able to *see* where you're going.

Question
Next, after you survey, but before you start reading, think about some questions that the survey might have raised in your mind. "So, what *is* the big deal about the War of 1812? Why do I have to know about it? Who fought in this war? What was at stake? How long did it last?"

Try to make some connections to things you already know. "Let's see. This was about 35 years after the Revolutionary War (1776) that established the United States as a separate country. Why were we already fighting another war so soon? What did we have to fight about?" And there are probably questions at the end of the chapter that might suggest other questions to you, things you might want to know about.

The idea is that you will be setting up questions in your mind--things *you* are curious about, things *you* wonder about, things *you* want to know. These are not the teacher's questions, not your friend's questions, and not the book's questions. They are *your* questions so that when you read, you will have a stake in the reading. **You will be more active and curious because you will be looking for answers to *your* questions to make connections in your own mind.**

Okay, you've surveyed the pages and formulated some questions in your head. This might have taken you all of five or six minutes. Is this time wasted? No way! Now, when you actually start to read, you will be able to read faster and with better comprehension than previously.

Read
What do you do when you read? That is up to you. Some people find it best to read through the pages from beginning to end to get the big picture in mind and see how all the pieces of the section fit together. This is good.

It is also good to form mental pictures of what you are reading. If there are pictures in the book, study those to help fix the images with the words.
Certainly, you will be looking for the answers to your own questions as you read. And you will be connecting old knowledge you already have to the new information you're reading about. New questions might come up as you read—things you don't understand,

something that is confusing. **In those cases, you might want to jot down a question to ask in class. If your mind wanders, you will gently tug it back, retrace anything you might have missed and go on. This is all good active reading.**

It is also very good to outline or take notes as you read. (In college, when you own the books, you can highlight, underline, or make notations in the margin of your books as you read.) This is taking the term "active reading" one step further, because you are physically active—taking notes—while you're reading. Studies have shown that the more ways you interact with the material, the more likely you are to remember it. In other words, if the information is coming in through your hands, through the act of writing it down, as well as through your eyes as you read it, it will be more fixed in your mind. If you don't own the books, and therefore, can't write in them, you can take notes in your notebook as you read. (More about this later in a note taking section.)

Recite
A third way to interact with the material is to recite it. Here are some ways to have a chance to recite the material.
- **After you read, go to the questions at the end, and mouth or recite the answers.**
- **Call a friend who has the same assignment and ask each other the questions.**
- **One of the very best ways to learn something is to teach it to someone else.** If your friend is confused about some concept in the reading, explain it to him or her. Go back to that part in the chapter and teach it to your friend. Reciting it this way will help you to understand it better.

Review
And finally, review! Review your notes by reading over them. **Review all the same things you surveyed in the chapter to begin with--those chapter headings and subheadings, the italicized words, the things in the boxes, etc. But they should all make sense to you now.** You should know what each one means because you have *learned* the information. You have added new knowledge and have connected it to what you knew before. You are now just a little bit smarter.

Assignment #10:

Practice using the SQ3R method.

Apply the SQ3R method to a reading assignment in one of your classes, such as social studies or science. Faithfully follow each of the steps—survey, question, read, recite, review. Then write down an analysis of how it went, answering these questions:

1. How long did it take you to do the whole SQ3R procedure?
   _____

2. Were you more involved and interested in the reading than usual?
   _____

3. Which part of the procedure did you think was the most helpful? Why?
_____

4. Which part did you find least important or helpful and why?
_____

5. Do you think you will retain the information that you read better than usual?
_____

6. Will you use this procedure again?
_____

STUDY SKILLS THAT WORK—TAKING NOTES

Another part of being an active learner is note taking. But there is a big difference between being a secretary and being a boss. A secretary simply writes down whatever the boss says without thinking about it. It's the boss who understands the big picture, who decides what is important and what's not, and who reaps the bigger rewards.

An active learner is not just taking dictation. An active learner is the boss, thinking about the material, making decisions about what is important, relating the information to something he/she already knows, questioning some parts of it. And it is the boss who will reap the rewards in terms of greater understanding and knowledge in the end.

One effective way to take notes is the Cornell system, developed at Cornell University many years ago. This system involves drawing a vertical line down the length of a page one-third of the way across it. **To the right of the page, in the widest two-thirds, you will take notes on what you think is important about what the teacher is saying or what you think is important in your textbook.**

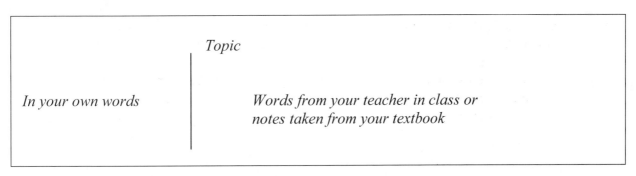

Later, within a few hours, when you review your notes, you will write key words or short personal restatements in the narrow left hand column. This forces you to re-read your notes and to summarize or consolidate what you've learned.

You learn more if you think through something and then put it in your own words. If you then say it aloud (recite it) you will have used three different ways for the information to get into your brain—visually, through your hand while writing it, and orally.

This technique can be used for taking notes from textbooks or for taking notes in class. But, of course, the best possible way to be an active learner is to do both.

High school teachers and college professors will usually assign reading and then follow up with a lecture or discussion about the reading. There is nothing more boring or incomprehensible than sitting through a lecture in which you have no idea what the teacher is talking about, because you didn't do the reading before class.

If you read, take notes, and have some questions ready about things you don't understand before you walk into the classroom, then all of a sudden that chapter means something when the teacher starts discussing it. This is because:
- The information sounds familiar and interesting, because you've already been thinking about it yourself.
- Taking notes in class won't be so difficult, because you'll know you already have written down a lot of the same information; so you don't need to write it down again.
- You can use the time in class to really listen and absorb what the teacher is saying.
- Watch how impressed your teacher will be when you ask a good, insightful question based on the material.

To further integrate what you've read with what the teacher is saying, one thing to do is only take reading notes on the left pages of your notebook, for example, and put class notes on the right pages. So, theoretically, information about the same topics will be next to each other in your notebook—textbook information on the left, teacher information on the right. When you go back to review, you can take it all in at a glance—teacher notes, text notes and your own summaries of it all. This actually is a time-saver.

Your notebook

My Reading Notes from Chapter on *Photosynthesis*			Notes Taken during Class on *Photosynthesis*	
My own words	Words, concepts, important ideas from textbook		My own words	Teacher's words, emphasizing things we should know

"Doesn't it take a lot of time to take all those notes after you read or while you're reading and *then* to go back and write it all in your own words? Because I just don't have that kind of time," you might say. Yes, it takes some time. It takes more time at first, until you get used to it, but it saves you time in the long run because:
- When you go to study for the test, you will have already reviewed your notes at least once.

- Your own words will mean more to you than whatever the book or teacher might have said.
- And best of all, you're more likely to have learned it, which means your grade on that material is probably going to be better than usual.

It's your decision.

Clues from teachers

Just as there are clues in textbooks about what is important (headings and sub-headings, words in bold, information in boxes, etc.) there are also clues from teachers as to what they think you should especially pay attention to and learn. These things should go into your notes. Teachers emphasize what is important in ways such as these:

- They will say:
    1. The most important thing is . . .
    2. Three crucial factors are . . .
    3. Remember these points . . .
    4. The point is . . .
- They repeat things.
- They put important information on the board or overhead projector.
- They get excited about certain things.
- They will say, "This will be on the exam."
- They will give you an outline or study guide.
- They will ask questions in class or give quizzes on information they think is particularly important.

Develop Your Own Shorthand

Teachers talk fast. Sometimes even if you've done the reading and taken notes on it, there is so much material to get through that the teacher just starts off like a rocket and keeps going. You need to have some shorthand strategies to use to keep up. Eventually, you will develop your own—a group of symbols and abbreviations that are meaningful to you. But here are some common ones that you might want to start practicing for that day when you walk into a class and the teacher blasts off.

w/	with	b/c	because
&	and	>	greater than
<	less than	=	equals
*	important	***	really important
bldg	building	→	leads to
info	information	def	definition
vs	against	gov	government
?	don't understand	???	really don't understand
ex	example	$	money/dollars

Reach for College!

Assignment #11:

Practice the Cornell Method of Note Taking.

Practice using the Cornell note taking system:
- from your reading
- from class

This means that after you read an assignment, you will take some time to take notes on it on the right two-thirds of a piece of paper in your notebook. Later, you will summarize or rephrase your notes on the left one-third of the page.

Similarly, during class, you will also take notes on the lecture or discussion on right two-thirds of the page, and later, in the evening, you will review your notes and summarize the class lecture notes in your own words on the left one-third. Practice this for one week or for the length of one unit or chapter in a class. Then evaluate.

1. Did the note taking system make learning easier or more interesting? _____

2. Was it easier to recall the information? _____

3. Was studying for the test easier? _____

4. Did you get a better grade than usual on the test? _____

5. Discuss in class how the Cornell note taking system worked or didn't work for you.
   _____

STUDY SKILLS THAT WORK—TAKING TESTS

You've been taking tests for at least 10 to 12 years. You probably have patterns of how you approach tests. These might range from panic accompanied by nausea to peaceful preparedness. The point of this section is to make you aware of your patterns and to help you critique them. In other words, you should look at how you study for tests and determine whether that works for you or not.

In high school teachers do many things to help students along. For tests, teachers will give you study guides. They will review before the test. They will give big hints about what's on the test. They will remind you several times to study for the upcoming test. They will give you time in class to prepare for it.

In college, you are much more on your own—no reminders, no helpful reviews that give you an idea of what to study, no study guides, no class time to prepare. So what can

you do? **You can start to get ready for college now.** Here are some suggestions that will help you improve your grades now, and will make things easier for you next year.

Don't study at the last minute.
This seems obvious. But . . . how much do you think your brain is really going to retain if you are stuffing it full of facts at the very last minute when it's nervous anyway?

Study a little bit each night for a week or a few days before a test.
In college your professors will give you a syllabus, which is a listing of what is going to be done every day in the class, when assignments are due, and when there are tests. So you will have plenty of advance warning about when tests are coming. Even in high school, teachers will usually give you about a week's warning or more on when to expect a test. If you know in advance, why wait until the night before or the hour before to prepare for it? If you go over your notes, read and answer the questions at the end of the chapter, and are able to do this when you are not panicked, you will remember more of it. It's as simple as that.

Try to anticipate what the questions will be.
This is not as crazy or as hard as it sounds. You have your notes. You've been paying attention in class. You know what has been emphasized. You can read a whole list of questions and important terms at the end of the chapter that the textbook authors have determined are the things they want students to remember. Study all those things.

Don't stick your head in the sand and say, "Oh, I hope he doesn't ask that!" Instead, assume that he will ask that and prepare for it. If it's the Kreb's cycle, then practice writing out the Kreb's cycle from memory. If it's a particular essay question, then outline and write out the answer to the question. **There is nothing that says you can't practice writing the answer before a test.**

Create your own study guide.
No study guide? Make up your own. Make it up a few days before the test. Write down all the important points and terms on a piece of paper and carry it around with you. When you have a couple of minutes, while waiting for the bus or for your sister to get out of the bathroom, or when you have that substitute in math who gives you a study hall, pull out your study guide and put your time to good use by reviewing what's on it.

Know what kind of test it's going to be.
If it's primarily an objective test, meaning multiple choice, true/false, and fill-in the blank questions, then you will want to study details, dates, facts, names, terms, formulas. You can do this by making a list of them, covering up the answers and quizzing yourself until you learn them.

But if it's going to be an essay test, you are going to want to know broader things, like tracing the history or development of something, causes and effects, trends, comparing and contrasting, analyzing or explaining something. The best way to prepare for this is to make study maps. Try to anticipate what the possible questions might be and then brainstorm the answers. Write the question in the middle of a page, look through your notes and the textbook and map the answers around the question, making sure to list details you want to use to support your points. Then use memory devices to help you remember your points and supporting details.

Study with a friend.
One of the best ways to learn something is to recite it or teach it to someone else. *If* you and a friend can stick to the task of studying, then get together to quiz and explain things to each other. You can also try to guess what the questions are going to be and compare notes to make sure what you are studying is accurate.

Sleep and eat well before a test.
This makes perfect sense, but too many students spend the night before an important test cramming for it instead of sleeping. Then they get up late, rush to school without breakfast and spend the test time concentrating more on the rumbles in their stomachs than on the test questions. Your brain can perform at its best when it's rested and has some energy in the form of calories to use.

If you have extra time after you have finished the test, turn it over and wait.
Let your brain relax for a minute. Sometimes, just that moment of letting down your guard will allow that elusive answer you couldn't think of to drift into focus. After a couple of minutes, turn the test back over and read over some of your answers. That is when you might discover that you left out an important word or two from the topic sentence of your essay question or you forgot to make an answer a negative number by adding the minus sign.

When you get the graded test back, analyze your mistakes.
Too many students look only at the grade when they get a test back, and then stuff it in their backpack, never to look at it again. One of the best ways to improve in any area of life is to learn from your mistakes. Everyone makes mistakes. The greatest of geniuses make mistakes, but part of what makes them so smart is that they look at what they did wrong so they won't make the same mistake the next time.

Look over your test. Did you miss a lot of true/false questions? Did you know the answer, but were tripped up on the wording of the question? If that is the case, you will know next time to concentrate particularly on reading the true/false questions very carefully. Was your topic sentence correct on the essay, but you lost points by not supporting your answer with enough details? So next time you'll know to concentrate on studying the details on your study map more thoroughly. Did you lose points because your handwriting or your spelling wasn't accurate enough on the fill-in the blanks? Next time you can print and you will make sure to study the spelling of the terms too.

STUDY SKILLS THAT WORK—STUDYING FOR MID-TERMS AND FINAL EXAMS

Whereas in high school you are given many tests, in college often there is only a mid-term, a final exam, and maybe a term paper in a class; and that is *all* you are graded on. Therefore, the pressure on each of these exams is great. It is a good idea, then, to learn how to organize and to study well for these kinds of tests while you are in high school, when these mid-terms and finals are not weighted so heavily.

All the same rules apply to studying for mid-terms and finals as apply to studying for any test, only you have to approach your studying in a more organized way and you have to start earlier because there is more to review.

 Reach for College!

Gather and organize your materials.
For each chapter that you will be tested on collect your reading and class notes, handouts, any memory aids (such as flash cards or concept maps) you've made yourself, study guides, homework, and previous tests or quizzes on this chapter. Put them all in one pile. Do this for each of the chapters you will be studying.

Make a study time schedule.
Figure out how long you have until the exam and how many chapters you have to review and divide up the studying accordingly. For example, if you have two weeks and ten chapters to review, then you could plan to study one chapter each weekday night, reserving a couple of days right before the exam to go over everything or the hardest things one more time.

This should not be first-time learning; this is reviving your thoughts about things you should already know. It shouldn't take you as long as the first time you were learning it. **The purpose of final exams, after all, is to consolidate what you've learned, to give you a chance to see the overall picture, to see how it all fits together, to really connect together all this new information in a meaningful way.**

Here are some other techniques that students have found helpful in reviewing for finals:
- Use a highlighter to highlight your notes or outlines to help remember the important things.
- Write up new notes or study guides just hitting the high points that will stimulate you to remember all the other facts that go together.
- Use different colored pens to underline things of different levels of importance.
- Answer all the questions at the end of the chapters to make sure you haven't missed anything.
- Turn to the index in the textbook and, if you've read everything from page 1 to 150, for instance, then quiz yourself to see if you are familiar with every index item that refers to those pages. If not, turn to that page and learn it. (This is a good one to do with friends and keep score.)

Assignment #12:

How do you study for tests? Is that working?
Answer the following questions about how you currently study for tests.

1. When do you study for a test? (You might say, for example, "one hour before," "the night before," "a little bit every night for a week before," "never.")
_____

2. How long do you study, generally?_____

3. What are some techniques that you use? (For example, flash cards, re-reading the chapter, covering up notes and memorizing them, writing out sample questions and answering them, memorizing study guide, etc.)
_____

_____

4. Do you study with someone else? _____

5. Do you change your study habits according to which class you are being tested in? _____

6. If you have time at the end of a test, do you go back over it and check your answers? _____

7. When you get a graded test back, do you analyze what you missed and why? _____

8. Are you satisfied with your test grades in all your classes? _____

9. Would you like to improve? _____

After having read the pages above giving you suggestions on successful test taking, think about the answers you have provided above. In what areas could you use some new strategies?

_____

_____

_____

USE WHAT WORKS FOR YOU

Let's be realistic. **No one is going to do all of the things listed in this chapter.** You can be a fine student and do only half or some of the things suggested. Everyone has to find out what works best for themselves and stick with that.

But as you approach a new chapter, a scary test, or your least favorite class, look back over the things in this chapter and try one or two of the suggestions as an experiment to see how they work for you. Maybe you'll discover that taking notes in the Cornell system really improves your grades. Maybe you find that surveying a chapter before diving into the reading works great to get your mind set up for reading, but the reciting part just doesn't do anything for you. Fine. **Use what works; forget the rest. The point is figuring out what works best for you to make you the best student you can be.**

Then stick with it. It will pay off. Hard work always does. Anything worth doing is difficult. If it weren't difficult, then everyone in the world would have been able to do it by now. But you have something not everyone in the world has, and that is the determination to try your hardest for something that will make you a better person in the end.

STAY ORGANIZED—READ THE SYLLABUS

In one very specific way, college is easier than high school, and that way involves organization. Most college professors will give you a syllabus for the course on the first day of class. What is a syllabus? A syllabus is a guide to the class. (See a sample syllabus on the following pages.) The syllabus usually includes:
- Course objectives/description—what it is you will learn.
- What will be required of you in terms of tests, quizzed, papers, etc.
- Attendance policies and other housekeeping items.
- The names of the books you will use.
- The office hours of the professor and the location of his or her office.
- Outline of dates of the class and what the topics will be on those dates.
- When tests, quizzes, presentations and papers are due.

In other words, in a few pages that the professor hands out on the first day, you have a whole view of what the semester will be like in that class. In high school, the longest view of things you have is usually a week or at most a month. The teacher might say on Monday that you will be having a test on Wednesday. This doesn't give you much time to prepare. In, college, however, you often have a total overview of the semester from the first day.

This is a big help for organizing your time and effort in the class. Keep the syllabus handy and put all significant dates into your planner. If there are things you should buy that are listed on the syllabus, such as a science kit or a certain kind of notebook, you can put that on a list to pick up at the bookstore.

Keep everything pertaining to each class in a separate notebook or folder, so when it's time to study for that class or find something related to that class, you will know right where to look and not have to waste time searching your whole backpack or desk.

Sample Syllabus
2126 CONTEMPORARY LITERATURE 1945 to the PRESENT
Professor Hammond
Summer Session

8:00-9:55 P.M. Tuesday and Thursday
Room H-102
Office: H-102
Office Hours: 7:00-8:00 PM Tuesday and Thursday and by appointment
Required Texts:
Literature: *The Evolving Canon.* Sven Birkerts (1996) Second Edition, Boston: Allyn and Bacon
The Stranger, Albert Camus
The Bluest Eye, Toni Morrison
Won't Take Nothing for My Journey Now, Maya Angelou
Short Stories and Poems (class handouts)

Materials:
Journal folder, writing materials. Recommended: Thesaurus, Dictionary and MLA Handbook for Writers of Research Papers (not essential to purchase.)

Course Description:
Contemporary Literature: 1945 to the Present offers an opportunity to explore a rich multitude of voices which have contributed to the second half of the 20th century. The readings will juxtapose genres of novel, drama, short story and poetry to explore themes of powerlessness and empowerment, oppression and freedom, despair and hope. In a literary canon continually evolving, the world of literature reflects issues and concerns about the complexities and multiplicities we are now challenged to face. The famous poet Rilke suggests "we must learn to love the questions themselves."

As part of the college's core curriculum, this course investigates the following questions:
What are our present ways of understanding ourselves and the universe?
How do we deal with conflicts in our ways of understanding?
How do we decide what we value?
How do we decide how to live our lives?

Attendance:
Class participation is an integral part of the course. Keep absences to a minimum; more than two absences are considered excessive. Please save absences for emergencies. Absences do not excuse students from due dates or other assignments.

Evaluation:
The three major papers will compose 70% of the student's grade. The formal written work will consist of three papers, with a suggested minimum length of 4-5 pages for each paper. Papers are double-spaced and typed.

Classroom participation in discussion, group response work, and Reflection Journals will determine 20% of your final grade.

Presentations will be evaluated at 10% of your grade. For presentations, each student w ill select a contemporary writer for presentation to discuss with the class. The presentations will include:
1) The context of the writer's work.
2) The current recognition of the writer.
3) The perceived significance of the writers' contributions.
4) The appeal of the writer and reasons for your choosing him or her.
5) The selection of an excerpt or pieces of poetry or prose from the writer's work.

Late Materials:
Students are expected to meet deadlines for formal papers. Later materials lower the grade for the particular paper at the instructor's discretion, unless the student has made arrangements in advance.

Schedule:
6/17   Course Introduction
6/19   Birkerts: Fictional Worlds, p 1-70
       Louis Jenkins, Guy De Maupassant
       Gabriel Garcia Marquez
       Bessie Head
6/24   Birkerts: Fiction, p. 71-162
       Delmore Schwartz, Frank O'Connor
       Junichiro Tanizaki
       Isak Dinensen, "The Blue Jar"
       James Joyce, "The Dead"
6/26   Eudora Welty, "A Worn Path"
       William Faulkner, "Wash"
       Milan Kundera, "The Hitchiking Game"
       John Updike, "Separating"
       Luisa Valenzuela, "I'm Your Horse in the Night"
       Amy Hempel, "In the Cemetery Where Al Jolson is Buried"
7/1   Albert Camus, *The Stranger*

7/3	Albert Camus, *The Stranger*
7/8	Birkerts: Selections from Poerty (To be assigned)
7/10	poetry selections
	Paper #1 due
7/15	Poetry Student Selections
7/17	Poetry Student Selections
7/22	A poet's career: Adrienne Rich
	Birkerts: 721-745
7/24	Poetry Presentations/Students
7/29	Maya Angelou: *Won't Take Nothing for My Journey Now*
7/31	**Paper #2 due**
8/5	Toni Morrison: *The Bluest Eye*
8/7	Toni Morrison: *The Bluest Eye*
8/12	**Presentations/Students**
8/14	**Presentations/Students**
	Paper #3 due

Assignment #13

Interpreting a Syllabus

Look over the sample syllabus above and answer the questions below:

1. What is a syllabus? _____

_____

2. Where and when do you get one? _____

From the sample syllabus:
3. What is the course name? _____

4. What is the course number? _____

5. What are the professor's office hours? _____

6. Where is her office? _____

7. How many books are required for the course? _____

8. What materials are required? _____

9. What materials are recommended? _____

10. How many absences does this professor consider to be excessive? _____

11. What will comprise 70% of a student's grade in this course? _____

12. How long are the papers supposed to be? _____

13. What will comprise another 20% of the grade? _____

14. On what days does the class meet? _____

15. When is the first paper due? _____ Approximately how long is that after the course starts? _____

16. How many days in class is Albert Camus' *The Stranger* discussed? _____

17. When is the second 4-5 page paper due? _____ Approximately how long is that after the first paper? _____

18. Would you like to take this course? _____

ADOPT AN ATTITUDE OF SUCCESS FOR THE ACADEMIC TRANSITION

The attitude you bring to your classes and to your interactions with your professors will make *all the difference* in your success in college. College is different from high school; and therefore, you should be different too.

One of the biggest differences is that everyone at college is an adult. Okay, maybe you *just* passed into adulthood, but everyone now considers you an adult. That means your attitude should be one of cooperation, partnership and mutual respect with other adults. The other adults at college are the administrators, the staff, the professors, and your fellow students. In short, everyone at college is an adult.

In high school you might have felt a certain rebellion or a bit of an adversarial relationship with the administrators and teachers when they enforced rules and policies. But in college there are many fewer rules and a lot less enforcement. The adults at college don't feel it's their responsibility to tell you what to do and where to go. They leave that up to you since you are now an adult, an equal. But they also expect that you will act responsibly, act like the adult you are, and do the right things.

The right things include:
- Learning the policies and procedures for getting things done at your college and following those (such as how to register for classes, get your financial aid, etc.)
- Going to class and participating in class.
- Doing the reading and writing necessary to succeed in all of your classes.
- Treating everyone on campus with the same respect that you expect for yourself.

This attitude of respect and taking responsibility will carry you a long way. Taking responsibility in your primary "job" of being a student means that if you register for a class, you will do all the necessary work for that class to the best of your ability. If you find you are falling behind or having trouble understanding the concepts, you will ask the professor for suggestions,

or for help—not the day before the exam, but when you first realize you're having trouble. An attitude of respect means that you will approach and treat everyone on campus as an equal and as you would wish to be treated. **If you sincerely adopt these attitudes, then you cannot and you will not fail.**

College is a wonderful opportunity for personal growth and for expanding your understanding of the world and of your chosen career field. Take advantage every day of the knowledge and new experiences being offered to you to become the person you are meant to be!

"I assume that if students are in my class, they're here to learn. I emphasize hard work. It's hard work that separates the so-called geniuses from the also-rans."
~Abdulalim Shabazz, Professor of Mathematics

Chapter Five

"My mother taught me that nothing worthwhile is gained without hardships or determination."
~Dorothy Dandridge

MAKE A SUCCESSFUL EMOTIONAL TRANSITION TO COLLEGE

In this chapter you will:
- Understand that, in addition to the social and academic transitions, you will also be making an emotional transition to college.
- Know that, as with the other transitions, this one will take several months and can be difficult at first, but you can prevail.
- Learn ways to help yourself through the emotional transition to college.

BE AWARE OF THE EMOTIONAL TRANSITION TO COLLEGE AND HELP YOURSELF TO SUCCESS

There is one more important transition you should be aware of as you make the adjustment to college, and that is the emotional transition. Since this is one that works inside of you, it can do a number on your head and heart. It is unlike the social transition which is plain to see in the shape of your new friends and the time you spend socializing. And it is unlike the stacks of new books and the growing number of papers on your desks that signify the academic transition. The emotional transition has no outward signs. It is invisible, yet it is often so powerful it can derail you if you're not careful.

This is how you might feel the emotional transition:
- You might feel homesick—missing family and familiar things back home.
- You might feel pulled by family issues at home.
- You might miss girlfriends, boyfriends or just regular friends back home.
- You might feel academically unprepared and inadequate.
- You might feel socially uncomfortable or out of place—the culture and people at college are so different from anything you've known before.
- You might wonder about your new identity—who you are becoming.
- You might feel sad, depressed and overwhelmed by all the new things and feel that you can't cope.

If all this sounds like a lot to deal with, you're right. It is. **The changes you go through in the emotional transition to college are big changes. But there are three very important things to remember:**

    1) Everyone experiences those same feelings whether they talk about them or not.
    2) It will be rough going at times, but you'll make the adjustment within a few months.
    3) If you stick with it, you'll get through it and be a stronger person because of it (and a college-educated person!)

HOMESICKNESS IS REAL BUT SHORT-LASTING

If you have never spent much time away from home before, then you will probably experience some homesickness at college. Homesickness might not hit you right away. In the initial whirlwind at college and all the new things to absorb, you might not miss the familiar things and people of home at first. But after you've been at school a couple of weeks, you're likely to start thinking more and more about the folks back home and wishing you were there. This is all entirely normal and it happens to just about everyone.

At first you might not recognize it as homesickness. You might just find that you aren't sleeping well because you don't hear the usual sounds of home outside your door or you don't like the food at college because you miss the cooking at home. You might feel vaguely uncomfortable with all the new people you're meeting because it's more work to get to know these people and to let them get to know you than it is to just hang out with people who have known you for a long time. These are signs of homesickness.

Later, you might begin to feel that the dearest sight for your eyes would be for your mom or your brother to walk into the room. You might yearn to see the familiar sights of the neighborhood or smell the aromas from home. You might even begin to miss the things that you didn't like so much about home—the familiar door-slamming fights between your sisters, or the TV constantly blaring from the kitchen. Suddenly everything from home seems like the best, most genuine, and important thing in the world. You understand the expression that your heart "aches" to see and hear and touch those things again.

Yes, homesickness can feel like a kind of sickness. And like an illness, it can affect all the other areas of your life, causing you not to enjoy your new friends or making you not want to do your school work.

You've got be strong though. This is where it gets tough and where you have got to be tough too. Understand that homesickness doesn't last long. Yes, it is painful while you're going through it, but chances are very good that by the end of the first semester, you'll be more than ready to return to college in January. It will be wonderful to see your family and old friends and to sleep in your own bed at Thanksgiving or for winter break. But after that you'll probably start to realize that you feel more at home at college than you do at home. And then you will realize that you have made the transition.

So what can you do to help yourself through the phase of homesickness? First, acknowledge what you're feeling. Say to yourself, "Man, I am *really* homesick. I miss everyone *so* much." Sometimes, just naming and accepting a problem helps us to cope with it.

Second, call home, and talk to the folks you miss. Sometimes part of what you are feeling is that you're worried about people at home, or you just want to be reassured by hearing their voices. Ask them about what's going on and get news about relatives and the neighborhood. Many times, you will find that they are doing fine and are more concerned about how you're doing. So, tell them how you're doing. Tell them what you have accomplished, who you've met, what you've done lately. Tell them you miss them, but you're doing okay. This will reassure them too.

Third, be determined to stick with it. The biggest favor you can do for yourself is to get through this. If necessary, just promise yourself to stick with it for one more day or one more week. And then promise yourself one more week again. The weeks will actually move along quickly. Even though it feels tough as you're going through it, you'll look back on it as just one small part of the transition to being a bigger, more mature person. You'll be glad you persisted.

YOU MIGHT FEEL PULLED BY FAMILY ISSUES AT HOME

In addition to homesickness, in which everything from home begins to seem sweet and desirable, you might also experience feelings of guilt related to people at home. This occurs in many cases when things at home aren't just as they should be and you feel responsible for being a support to one or more people at home. Maybe it's a younger brother or sister you left behind to what you know will be instability in the house. Maybe it's a sick mother or grandmother who leaned on you for years. Maybe it's a whole series of folks you usually help out and who will have a harder time without you there.

You might also feel guilty about all the money being spent on you for your education. When you think about the thousands of dollars that are going toward this, you hope you can live up to everyone's expectations.

This is a hard situation, no doubt about it, and your feelings are understandable. However, a critical thing that you must keep always in the front of your mind is that if you are there with them, you are not going to be doing what you need to do to help them in the long run. If you were to stay at home and work in a typical high school graduate's job, you would earn about $15,000-$25,000 a year. If you stay in college and later work in a typical college graduate's job you will earn more than twice that--$35,000-$57,000 a year. Since many of your family's problems might be helped if they had more money, doesn't it seem wiser to stick it out and get to the point where you can *really* assist them?

Plus, staying at home is not going to help you. You need to think about yourself too. Certainly there have been students who were accepted to college, went for a semester and then decided they needed to go back to their families to help out. Here is what they say four or five years later.

"Now that I'm almost 25, I have nothing but regrets. I'm in a lousy job that's going nowhere and my family is the same as it's always been—no changes. I tried so hard to do what everyone expected of me to help out and yet I feel it hasn't really made a difference. Everything's about the same. And I neglected what I wanted for myself. Now I feel like all the doors are closed to me. I wish I was going somewhere in my life. I still have some dreams, but I think it's too late for me."

At some point, the people at home who you feel are pulling you back, need to let you do what you can do for yourself, and they need to do what they can for themselves too. Yes, of course, you love them and want to help and protect them, but years fly by quickly. If you stick with your goals and your time frame, you can soon be there for them but in a much better place to actually make some real changes for them.

For younger brothers and sisters, if you stay in college you will be the pioneer that will make it easier for them to go to college. Being this role model and helping pay for them go to college is the key to a better life for them too. What greater gift can you give them?

So, think about the long term. Think about where you would be four years from now if you went back home to help out. And also think about where you'll be four years from now if you stay in college. Mature decision-making involves this sort of long-term thinking and planning. And mature dedication and perseverance will take you to your goals.

YOU MIGHT MISS FRIENDS YOU'VE LEFT BEHIND

You might be separated from boyfriends, girlfriends and just plain friends who are very dear to you when you go to college. It is another difficult part of the emotional transition to college. These bonds can stretch but they don't have to break. It is up to you. Call your friends, email them, or write them.

It is also true, though, that you will be meeting lots of new people and making lots of new friends. Some of these new friends might, after a very short period of time, become close friends. In all the intensity of new experiences on campus, this is not unusual, so don't be afraid of it. Welcome this, and remember that you can bring new people into your circle and still keep your old friends. Both are dear; both enrich you.

Sometimes, though, the new friends create friction with your old friends because your old friends feel your loyalty to them has been divided. This can feel hard for you as the person in the middle. Try to reassure both sets of friends and move on. Keep in mind that any friend who doesn't want you to expand and grow or a friend who doesn't want to accept your prior friends has to be questioned. Friends always should want the best and cause the least hassle for each other.

Boyfriends and girlfriends are special cases. It often happens that going away to college causes break-ups. This is because as you see a wider world, you realize that maybe you're not ready to be with just one person yet. Maybe you see that there are lots of good people out there who you might want to date. At the same time, you might have made promises to the person back home. Of course, this is all entirely your call and the decision-making involved can be one more source of inner turmoil during the first few weeks or months of the emotional transition.

But despite any upheaval you might experience, remember to keep your focus. Why are you at college? You're there to learn and to move, step by step, toward your goal. Don't let yourself get sidetracked and end up not accomplishing what you set out to do.

YOU MIGHT FEEL ACADEMICALLY UNPREPARED AND INADEQUATE AT FIRST

As we've said earlier in this book, it is very likely that you will come to college and have some academic catching up to do. It's not your fault, but the schools you attended might not have prepared you well enough for college. This means that for the first few classes you take in college you might feel that you are in over your head. You might feel that, compared to others in the class, you don't know enough and you are unprepared for what the class is demanding of you.

For example, the professor might regularly assign more reading in a week than you would have done in a month in high school. You might get papers back covered with red markings indicating problems with your writing. You might have holes in your knowledge—things that everyone else in your science class seems to assume as basic, but you were never taught. This can be very discouraging and make you feel inadequate, make you feel that you will never be able to survive academically at college.

Yes, it is discouraging that you might not have as good a background as other students. But students who have faced this very same problem have found out that gradually they *can* and *do* catch up. It takes hard work and determination. But it's been done by a lot of other students and you can do it too.

Keep in mind a few things. First, just because you're behind does not mean you are not smart. If the college admitted you, the college thinks you are smart enough to succeed there. The college sees your potential. The college wants you to succeed and wants to help you on your way to your goals. It's just that your starting block has been set a little behind the starting line. You've got to run faster and harder at first to catch up with everyone else. This is maddening and it will be hard work, but it can be done. You can do it.

Second, there are people to help you. People want to help you, so let them. Be open to asking for help, seeking it out and accepting it. This will speed up your learning process. Meet with and talk to your professors, tell them your situation, get suggestions, and follow through. Go to the tutoring center because that's what it's there for—to help students. Use it regularly. Talk to other students. Find out their tricks for doing the reading faster or for studying for certain types of tests.

Third, keep faith with yourself. Believe in yourself. Understand that the academics might be challenging at first but don't beat yourself up if you don't get it right away, if you can't read fast enough right away, or if your writing stinks at first. It will get easier and you will get better. Stick with it and not only will you survive, you will thrive.

YOU MIGHT FEEL OUT OF PLACE AT FIRST

If you are someone who has never moved around much except maybe into new neighborhoods in your own city, then you might be surprised to learn that every place is a little bit

different. Not only is the physical environment different, but sometimes the food and the way people talk and dress is different. Sometimes people's attitudes and what they do for work and fun are different. Colleges also usually strive to create a diverse student body, so there will be students from all over the place—the kinds of people you might not have ever encountered before. All these cultural differences are interesting to learn about and to see. But they can also make you feel a little out of place at first until you get used to them.

The college/university culture itself is probably also different from what you might have experienced in the past. It is an environment that is unique and set off, quite often, from the world of work and everyday things. Sometimes people call colleges "ivory towers." This is because professors and students at colleges are engaged in reading, writing and thinking about lofty thoughts and theories and not so much with practical, day-to-day realities. For most people, this is a huge change from what they're used to, so it feels strange at first.

Further, each college has its own particular culture. In most cases, individual colleges and universities have been around for decades and sometimes centuries. So they each have their own particular history, culture, traditions, words that refer to specific things, and ways of doing things. This is something else to get used to when you get to your college.

The combination of all these different cultures can make your head whirl trying to take in all the new sights, sounds, smells, thoughts and attitudes. That's okay. In fact it's wonderful! That's part of the thrill of the first few weeks. It's exciting and stimulating to step into any new world.

But sometimes you might feel a little uncomfortable at first, like you don't really fit in. Everything might seem alien and strange and you might feel a little off-balance. You might look around and feel that other kids seem to be fitting in better or easier than you. (That's not necessarily true. They might be looking at you and think you're the one who's cool and fitting in so well!)

As with the other transitions, these feelings will pass. It takes a few days or weeks to get used to everything that is new, but then you'll see how it all fits together. You will start feeling that this is your new reality and you'll probably start to like it. Most importantly, you will find your own niche, your own group of friends who all pretty much see the world the same way and that will increase your comfort level too.

If you're at a majority white campus and you haven't been around a lot of white people before, you might face some uncomfortable feelings beyond what they might be feeling. While the possibility is low that white students will physically harm you, there is a larger possibility that they might say things that hurt you psychologically or emotionally. This might be intended or unintended on their part.

Our society is so segregated, that chances are the white students haven't had a lot of exposure to African American students. Since part of the college experience is opening up to learning in all aspects of life, white students might want to learn about you and your experience of the world in dorm or social situations as well as in class. So they might ask you a lot of questions. At times they might seem to designate you as the "spokesperson for your race" or ask

Reach for College!

you stupid questions like "How often do you wash your hair?" or "Can you get sunburned?" or "Why do black kids always sit together in the cafeteria?"

These questions can be not only annoying, but can also be offensive. Feel your own way with this and consider the source. If the purpose of the questions seems to be to offend you or if they begin to sound like racial insults or slurs, then you should stand up for yourself, and walk away, or tell them to back off. Later speak to someone on the faculty or in the administration about this. All campuses now are extremely sensitive to racial intolerance and hatred and impose heavy penalties on students who engage in any kind of inappropriate behavior of this kind since it goes against everything that college is about.

If, on the other hand, the purpose of the question seems to be to honestly try to understand your point of view, you might want to answer the question in a way to educate the person, but then also inform them that you do not appreciate or are offended by this type of question and explain why. This, too, will help them understand you and your perspective better.

Of course, if the conversation feels okay to you, feel free to ask them questions you might have too. Open-mindedness and willingness to participate in the give and take of learning should be traits of all college students. Since we all need more tolerance and cross-cultural, cross-racial understanding in this country and in the world, these conversations, if they feel okay to all involved, can go a long way toward helping everyone feel a little closer.

YOU MIGHT WONDER ABOUT YOUR NEW IDENTITY—WHO ARE YOU BECOMING?

As everything seems to be wide open around you—all kinds of diverse people, new places to live, new hours, new foods, new attitudes, all kinds of new ways to live that are different from what you're used to—you'll find that you are exploring and trying out all these new things. That's good! That's what's supposed to happen!

One day you might hang out with the jocks and take on some of their identity and style. Another day you might hang out with the computer geeks and start talking about mega-bytes and pixels. A third day you might hang out with the campus environmentalists and start wearing their t-shirts. After awhile you might start to wonder, "Hey, who am *I* and how do *I* want to be?" This is all good, and all part of the process in the emotional transition.

How can you know what feels right unless you try out various identities? Exploring, talking, learning, trying new things is all part of the process of figuring out what you think is important and what you value and want to emphasize in your life. Learning about yourself and setting your priorities is an important part of growing up and the emotional transition to college.

Don't feel as if you've lost yourself if you're trying out lots of different things. Feel that you are finding yourself—finding out what you like and what's important to you because that is exactly what you're doing. This is a very good thing.

Feel good that you are driving your own development as a human being. In other words, you are directing how you are changing and growing. You are in control of what you explore

Reach for College!

and what you ultimately choose to value. You are in the process of creating something important and unique—you! And this part of the emotional transition is helping you to learn about yourself, know yourself and respect yourself. It's exciting and you should stand back every few weeks, notice the growth in yourself, and pat yourself on the back.

SUCCESS WITH THE EMOTIONAL TRANSITION TO COLLEGE HELPS YOU TO BECOME A BETTER, WISER PERSON

College is all about growing and becoming a bigger, wiser, more understanding person. It's about open-mindedness, learning about diverse people, places and ways of living. This learning goes on in the classroom and outside of it as well. The emotional transition helps you to expand your heart, mind and vision. Successfully navigating this transition is very important. It will make you a bigger, better person.

Assignment #14:

How will you navigate the emotional transition to college?

Though you won't know how you will actually feel until you get on to your college campus, what do you anticipate will be easiest and hardest for you in making the emotional transition to college? Think about the list below and write down your thoughts in answer to the questions.

Some of the issues you may confront in the emotional transition:
- You might feel homesick—missing family and familiar things back home.
- You might feel pulled by family issues at home.
- You might miss girlfriends, boyfriends or just regular friends back home.
- You might feel academically unprepared and inadequate at first.
- You might feel out of place at first—the culture and people at college are so different from anything you've known before.
- You might wonder about your new identity—who you are becoming.

1. I think what I may be able to cope with the easiest from the list above will be:

_____

_____

2. This will be easiest because I bring certain experience or strength to this new situation, This experience or strength is:

_____

_____

...*after Graduation*

3. I think what I may be hardest for me from the list above will be:

_____

_____

4. This will be hardest because:

_____

_____

_____

5. When the going gets tough, who can I call who I know will give me support to keep going?

_____   _____

6. When the going gets tough, what will I tell myself so I'll remember my goals and keep going?

_____

_____

_____

"Greatness is not measured by what a man or woman accomplishes, but by the opposition he or she has to overcome to reach his or her goals."
~Dorothy Height

Reach for College!

Chapter Six

"First forget inspiration. Habit is more dependable. Habit will sustain you whether you're inspired or not. Habit is persistence in practice."
~Octavia E. Butler, Bloodchild and Other Stories

MANAGE YOUR TIME

In this chapter, you will:
- Learn that "time management" means you control time instead of time controlling you.
- Analyze your use of time.
- Understand two important elements of time management: prioritizing and planning.
- Practice prioritizing.
- Practice planning for the accomplishment of a goal.
- See how changing your routine can give you more time.
- Establish a yearly calendar to help you organize and plan ahead.
- Establish a weekly calendar to help you prioritize and plan.

TIME MANAGEMENT IN COLLEGE IS CRUCIAL TO SUCCESS

Every first-year college student will tell you that the way you manage or don't manage your time in college can make or break you. **Good time management is cited by students and professors as probably *the* most important element in making a successful academic transition to college.** "Successful students know how to plan; they know how long it will take them to meet their daily and weekly goals. They do their research early, and seek out help as soon as they need it," according to one professor.

Time is a funny, invisible, elusive fact of life. We are not so aware of it until we are almost out of it. Ask students who have big homework projects due the next day, and they will tell you how much invisible time is weighing them down.

Sometimes time seems to go fast. And sometimes it creeps along. You feel like you had more time when you were young. And now you feel like you have less and less.

People approach time in different ways; they have different habits about time. There are those people who insist on being "on time," and who are never late with anything. Then, there are those who define themselves as "procrastinators," who are rarely on time with homework assignments or to meet you at the bus stop.

Since time is so elusive, impossible to grasp and hold on to, how can you manage it? "Manage" means "to exert control over, to make submissive to one's authority and discipline." In other words, **time management means that you harness and control time for your purposes. You control time instead of letting it control you.**

How can you begin to practice right now the time management skills that can make you successful in college? That's what this chapter is about.

Assignment #15:

How do I spend my time?

The idea behind this assignment is for you to begin to be conscious about how you use your time, because many people say they have *no* time available to them. Let's see if that is true. Use the 24-hour time sheet and note what you do each hour of a weekday for one 24-hour period. It will look something like this:

6:00 am	Asleep
6:30 am	Asleep
7:00 am	Wake up, shower, get dressed
7:30 am	Eat breakfast, watch cartoons
8:00 am	Leave for school
8:30 am-3:30pm	School
3:30 pm	Football/cheerleading/softball practice

A.M.
12:00 _____
12:30 _____
1:00 _____
1:30 _____
2:00 _____
2:30 _____
3:00 _____
3:30 _____
4:00 _____
4:30 _____
5:00 _____
5:30 _____
6:00 _____
6:30 _____
7:00 _____
7:30 _____
8:00 _____
8:30 _____
9:00 _____

P.M.
12:00 (noon)_____
12:30 _____
1:00 _____
1:30 _____
2:00 _____
2:30 _____
3:00 _____
3:30 _____
4:00 _____
4:30 _____
5:00 _____
5:30 _____
6:00 _____
6:30 _____
7:00 _____
7:30 _____
8:00 _____
8:30 _____
9:00 _____

9:30 _____	9:30 _____
10:00 _____	10:00 _____
10:30 _____	10:30 _____
11:00 _____	11:00 _____
11:30 _____	11:30 _____

Effective time management is one of the biggest stumbling blocks for many students. It's hard in high school. It's even harder in college. So, it would be a good idea to get a jump on things and learn how to manage your time wisely now, starting with analyzing how you use your time every day. Answer the questions below.

I spend most of my time _____ and _____.

I was surprised to see how *much* time I spend _____.

I was surprised to see how *little* time I spend _____.

I wish I spent less time _____.

I want to spend more time _____.

Dig deeper into your study of how you use your time.
Keep a time sheet (like the one above) of your activities for a week. Then answer the following questions:

I spend most of my time _____.

I was surprised to see how much time I spend _____.

I wish I spent less time _____.

I want to spend more time _____.

I could get more time for some things I want or need to do by _____
_____.

PRIORITIZE

One of the most effective time management tools, which will yield instant results, is prioritizing. **Prioritizing means putting things in order of importance or urgency.** Some people seem to do this instinctively. Other people find they need to train themselves to prioritize.

Let's say there is an emergency. A tornado has just blown down your house and your neighbors' homes. It's not hard for most people to prioritize the things that need to be done in this situation.

Number the following items in the order in which they must be done, in your opinion. (#1 should be completed first, #5 last.)

_____ Find shelter, clothing and food for the short term.

_____ Make sure everyone is safely out of the homes and give immediate medical attention to anyone who is hurt.

_____ Find shelter, clothing and food for the long term until the homes can be rebuilt.

_____ Call for assistance from the fire department or ambulance crews.

_____ Stay away from any live electrical wires or gas lines that may have been damaged until the authorities can verify the safety of them.

(For the priority list above, the numbers should be: 4,1,5,2,3.)

In a similar way good time management means looking at a list of things that need to be done in your day and putting them in order of what should be done first and what can wait until a little later. Highest on the list will be the most important or urgent things. Lower on the list will be the less important things or things that can wait, in case you don't get to them today.

Prioritize the following list by numbering the items in order of importance of what should be done first. (#1 should be completed first, #5 last.) It is Thursday at 8:00 P.M.

_____ Call friend to make plans for the weekend.
_____ Study for biology test to be given tomorrow.
_____ Shop for mother's birthday present. Her birthday is Sunday.
_____Write rough draft of English paper due Monday.
_____ Do math homework due tomorrow.

(The best priority list for above would be 4, 1, 5, 3, 2.)

When we sit back and look objectively at this list, it is fairly easy to see what should be done first and what can be put off until later. (No, calling your friend to make weekend plans does *not* come first.)

And yet **what frequently happens is that we do things not in order of what *should* come first, but in order of what we *want* to do first—and that is usually what we think is easiest.** It's much easier to call and chat with a friend or to go shopping than it is to face studying for that bio test or doing that math homework. (Either of the latter should have been first on your list, with the studying to be done when you are most alert.)

Reach for College!

So, **prioritizing** means not just listing what you have to get done and deciding the best order in which to complete it, but it **also means having the discipline to follow through** on your decision. Do what needs to be done first, then reward yourself with the easier things.

PLAN

A plan is any detailed scheme, program or method worked out beforehand for the accomplishment of a goal.

We all have many goals--large and small--that we think about off and on daily. Some are big, long-term, far-in-the-distance goals, such as graduating from college, going to law school and becoming a lawyer. Others are small goals that involve just looking ahead a day or a week into the future, such as to get an A on the next Spanish test. Then there are some goals in the middle—to graduate from high school with a 3.0 GPA, eligible for many scholarships. We might have the goal to lose ten pounds, to get a driver's license, or to learn to tap dance.

Any **goal that you can come up with will be easier to reach if you have a plan. The more detailed the plan and the more you break it down into little steps—small things you can do each day—the more likely you are to follow your plan.** In other words, if your goal is to apply for as many scholarships as possible, and all your plan says is "research scholarships and apply" chances are you will be so intimidated by all the myriad of places to look for scholarships and the huge number of applications you have to do that you will give up after the second day of trying.

But if your plan is detailed enough to break the task down into smaller pieces, you will be more likely to stick with it. So, your plan might say:
- Research scholarships (complete by February 1):
    1. Print list of scholarships I'm eligible for from FastWeb.
    2. Ask at church for scholarships they might offer
    3. Check www.rfchelp.org for latest scholarship offerings
- Apply for scholarships (Complete by April 1):
    1. Choose 10 of best possible scholarships that I qualify for & might get to apply for
    2. Write deadline dates on calendar
    3. Complete one application per week and send

A detailed plan like this only takes a few minutes to set up, but it gives you a specific "training schedule" to adhere to. It gives you clear goals that will give you a feeling of accomplishment for having completed them. You can also feel secure knowing that you will be able to fit it all in and get your work completed on time. Best of all, you will know that if you stick to your plan, you will be able to reach the goal you have set for yourself. **A plan is a road map through time that will take you to your goal.**

Assignment #16

Practice prioritizing and planning.

Prioritize:
1. Make a list of all the things you need to accomplish today. These might include things such as: homework assignments, chores or family responsibilities, community service or church obligations, filling out an application for employment or for college or for a scholarship.
2. Number the things you want to get done in order of importance or urgency.
3. As you accomplish them throughout the day, reward yourself by checking them off your list.

Priority order	Thing to be accomplished	Finished
_____	_____	_____
_____	_____	_____
_____	_____	_____
_____	_____	_____
_____	_____	_____
_____	_____	_____
_____	_____	_____

Plan:
Let's say your goal is to improve your grade point average. Define what steps need to be taken to reach this goal, then write out a detailed time plan for the accomplishment of this goal.

What **steps** need to be taken to reach this goal?

_____

_____

_____

_____

_____

Detailed **time plan** leading directly to goal:

_____

...after Graduation

_____
_____
_____
_____
_____

Choose another goal and write out a plan to reach it. Here are some suggestions of goals you might have:
- Get enough scholarship money that I won't have to have a job while I'm in college.
- Get my driver's license.
- Get a summer job or internship.

Steps to reach goal: (I need to complete . . .)   **Time Plan: (I will do it by . . .)**

_____   _____
_____   _____
_____   _____
_____   _____
_____   _____
_____   _____

SHORT-RANGE TIME MANAGEMENT FOR TODAY

Okay, okay . . . I've got all those medium-range and long-range things planned for. But, excuse me, I've got a time crunch *today*. First, there's practice right after school. I've got a 50-page reading assignment in English due on Friday. (50 pages. Right! Who is she kidding?) A chemistry test is breathing down my neck, and I'm working tonight from 7-9:30. Folks are jabbering to me about this college application and that scholarship application. Ain't no way all *this* is getting done!

Guess what? You're right! It's not all going to get done *today*. But, then again, it's not all due *tomorrow*. Sometimes everything seems to be crushing in on us so much that we get overwhelmed, feel like we're drowning, and give up. We throw up our hands and say, "This is too much! I surrender. I'm not doing *anything*."

But that's not going to get you where you want to go. When you have that overwhelmed feeling, the best thing to do is sit down, take five minutes and write down all the things you have to do. Here's our list. What absolutely has to be done *today*? Put an asterisk by those things. Then prioritize the list.

* __3__ Work 7-9:30

* __2__ Athletic practice 3:30-5:30

__4__ English reading (50 pages!!!)

* __1__ Chemistry test tomorrow

__6__ College applications

__5__ Scholarship applications (due next week)

Once you have decided what *has* to be accomplished today, you forget the rest. *Forget them?* Yes. That should drop your stress level about three notches.

Next, among the things you have to do today, decide which is most important. This will not necessarily be what you have to do first. Practice after school comes first in time sequence, but that Chemistry test is the most important because you are trying to get an A in Chemistry. Remember? So, you think about how long you estimate it's going to take you to study for that test and you look at the rest of the hours in your day and decide when that studying can happen.

Well, after you get home and shower and before you go to work, you usually sit down and watch a half an hour or so of Scooby Doo. Your brain hasn't been thinking Chemistry while you were at practice after school, so you could probably get in a decent half hour of studying then, instead of cartoons. And after work, when you usually spend an hour on the phone catching up on the day's events, there's some more time for Chemistry.

You figure you're going to have to do a *lot* of English reading tomorrow. But that's tomorrow when you won't have any Chemistry homework to face, and you don't have to work. That scholarship application could be fit in over the weekend. The college application isn't due until next month. You'll make a long-range detailed plan to take care of those.

This is time management—taking control of time and the things you have to do, so they don't control you.

CHANGING ROUTINES ADDS EXTRA TIME TO YOUR DAY

At this point in the school year, you pretty much know your schedule—where you have to be and for how long—six hours in school five days a week, two hours of practice after school, maybe three hours of work two nights a week. These are the blocks of time that you can't do much about.

But what about the other hours of the day or week? That's where establishing a new routine for yourself can gain you a lot of time. **A routine is simply a set of habits or a kind of schedule that you regularly go through.** If you kept a time sheet on your activities for a week, you can see your routines at a glance. Maybe you routinely watch TV at night from 8:00-9:30. Maybe you routinely eat a snack around 10:00 at night. Maybe you routinely oversleep and rush out of the house with your hair a mess.

If you feel you don't have enough time, think about your present routine. Where can you pick up an extra fifteen minutes or a half an hour each day? **By slightly changing one habit, one routine, for a half an hour a day, for instance, you can add two and a half hours to your week for something else**—a goal you might be working toward. By setting your alarm clock to go off ten minutes earlier, changing your routine only a little, you can have time to fix your hair before you rush out to the bus.

This is also good time management—changing old habits to take control of your life and your time.

YEARLY CALENDAR

One of the most effective ways to manage your time and to make planning easier is to carry and use a calendar. Use your school's calendar to write down all the important dates coming up in the whole school year. Use your church's calendar to write down all the important dates coming up for their year. Add friends' and family birthdays for the whole year. Write down all the deadlines you're trying to meet for college and scholarship applications. Having all these dates down in black and white will let you look ahead and see when you are likely to be busy and when you should prepare to have things done ahead of time.

Now, give yourself a little extra boost in planning ahead. Go back a week before all the birthdays and write in a reminder to yourself—"Mom's birthday in a week, get gift" or "Tracy's birthday in a week, get card." This way you will be prepared for the event, and chances are you won't be crushed for time at the last minute.

Go back two weeks before the college and scholarship deadlines and write reminders—"State application due in two weeks." "Coke Scholarship due in two weeks." These reminders will help you to budget time in those two weeks before the deadline to get those extra things done.

Using the calendar, you should be able to tell right away which weeks are going to be busier than others, and you can plan your time accordingly. If you can see you are going to have a horrendous week in the middle of March, maybe you could ask now for time off from work that week. If you can see there is going to be an impossible crunch in May, maybe you can plan to use one day of spring vacation to get some things done early. The important thing is to be able to look into the future and see the waves coming, before they hit you and knock you off your feet.

WEEKLY CALENDAR

A yearly calendar helps you plan for the long-range events. **A weekly calendar can help you organize your time for the short-term.**

It will probably be a little easier to organize your time in college than it is in high school because college professors usually give you the assignments for the whole week or even the whole semester at once in the form of a syllabus, which is basically an outline of the course. In high school, often teachers will only give you the assignment for the next day. If you have a heavy load of classes now and are having trouble getting everything done, explain to your teachers that you are trying to budget your time for the week and ask them to give you the assignments for the week on Monday.

Once you know what specifically is due and when, you can prioritize and plan. Write your plan in your calendar. If you are going to have to finish reading chapter 4 by Friday, divide up the pages in chapter 4, and write in your calendar how many pages you should read each night. If you are having a test in another class on Thursday, estimate how long it will take you to study for it, and block out your study time on Tuesday and Wednesday. If you are going to have to turn in your lab report on Friday, schedule a time right away with your lab partner to compare notes and write up the report.

By planning what you are going to do and when you are going to do it, you can be sure to get it all done, and you won't have to stay up until 1:00 AM on Thursday night, because so many things are due on Friday. You will have done a little bit all week to prepare for that busy Friday.

Assignment #17

Use a calendar to plan ahead.

You may have already started using a calendar. If so, check your calendar to see if you have items to add from question #1 below. Then add items from questions #2-4 to your calendar. If you haven't started a calendar, follow all of these steps.

1. Get or make a calendar for this year. Go through this yearly calendar and put in all of these items:
    - Important school dates—use the school system calendar and write in all holidays, teacher planning days, dates for Homecoming, Prom, Graduation, mid-term and final exams, etc.
    - Important family dates—birthdays, anniversaries, etc.
    - Important friend dates—birthdays, etc.
    - Important dates specific to you—recitals, camping trip with church youth group, sports practice times and game dates, your work schedule as far as you know it, choir practice and performance dates, etc.
    - SAT test date or dates you've registered for
    - Deadlines for applications to the colleges you are applying to

- Deadlines for scholarships you are applying to
- Any assignments you already know that are going to be due

2. Go back a week before all the birthdays and write in a reminder to yourself—"Mom's birthday in a week, get gift" "Tracy's birthday in a week, get card."

3. Go back two weeks before the college and scholarship deadlines and write reminders— "Tenn. State application due in two weeks" or "Coke Scholarship due in two weeks."

4. As you get homework assignments, write them into the calendar.

USE GOOD TIME MANAGEMENT TECHNIQUES AND DISCIPLINE TO REACH YOUR GOALS

Here are some quotes from first-year college students:
- "The biggest difference between high school and college is that there is a lot more work and a shorter time to do it."

- "In high school I did not have good time management skills. So now I am paying the price. In high school I would wait to the last minute to do reports, but in college waiting to the last minute is death. Every computer is in use or broken or every book I need is gone."

- "Time management is a science. First semester I had no time management skills. And my grades reflected that. I would tell high school seniors to establish time management skills as soon as possible before entering college. One of the key elements of time management is prioritizing."

Sharpen your time management skills right now to help your routines and habits work to your advantage. Not only will you feel less stressed by handling your time better, you will also be successful, through discipline, in reaching your goals.

"It doesn't matter what you are trying to accomplish. It's all a matter of discipline."
~Wilma Rudolph

Chapter Seven

"We must treat bad habits like enemies; fight them off until they are at bay. And, always be looking for where they might seek an opening for a sneak attack so that you can keep them at bay."
~Mildred Greene, Armchair Philosopher

"Take a stand! Aim to be healthy."
~Victoria Johnson, Author

MANAGE YOUR INDEPENDENCE & PERSONAL RESPONSIBILITIES

In this chapter, you will:
- Realize that you will be handling new and grown-up responsibilities now.
- Learn ways to step up to your new adult responsibilities that will lead to success in college and in your future life.
- Understand that you will now be on your own to take care of:
    1. Keeping your living space and clothes clean.
    2. Eating a good diet on a regular schedule.
    3. Staying healthy through eating well, getting enough sleep, exercising, and not engaging in risky behaviors.
    4. Controlling your personal safety.
    5. Managing your money.

HANDLING YOUR PERSONAL RESPONSIBILITIES WELL CAN START YOU ON A SOLID PATH TOWARD ADULTHOOD

Though you are officially "grown" and an "adult" when you turn eighteen and go to college, it's likely that there are many "adult-type" responsibilities you have not yet had experience with or had to deal with. These might include being completely responsible for:
- Keeping your living space and clothes clean.
- When, what and how you eat.
- Your health.
- Your personal safety.
- Your money, banking, and thousands of dollars of financial aid.

Most likely, you have been responsible for certain aspects of some of these things over the last few years. But, you've probably also had parents or other family members that you could fall back on to help you out with these things or who held the primary responsibility for supplying these things to you. If you go away to college you will start to bear the total responsibility for these things since you are physically separated from your family. But even if you stay at home and go to college, you will likely be much more independent and will take on many more of the responsibilities for your own life. This is as it should be.

This chapter is to acknowledge that you will now be stepping up to these new obligations and to give you a few tips about traps to avoid and ways to cruise through this transition in assuming your new responsibilities as an adult.

YOUR RESPONSIBILITY—KEEPING YOUR PERSONAL SPACE AND CLOTHES CLEAN

Your living space.

It's quite likely that you've been mainly responsible for keeping your room and clothes clean for years. You might have done this to your standards or to your family's standards. But now you will have to mesh this with your own and your roommate's standards. It helps if you both have similar ideas about the level of cleanliness in your dorm room. But if one of you is a neatnik and the other a slob, this can be a cause of tension. It's best to talk about this directly and try to reach some compromises or agreements about how to handle this. Remember that you will probably feel more organized and together if you keep things fairly organized and together in your personal living space.

Your clothes.

Clothes get dirty. They get wrinkled. They sometimes begin to smell. They need to be washed, dried, ironed, folded, and put away. These are the hard realities. For most college students, the task of doing the laundry is not what's difficult. What is hard is finding the time to do it. That is why you need to put that chore onto your "to do" list of time management tasks.

Of course, there are always ways of using your time wisely while the clothes are washing and drying. You can take your book and notebook to the laundry room and read or study while the machines are droning. You can use that time to clean up your side of the room. And there are tricks to shorten the process too, such as learning the times when the machines are usually free and doing your laundry then. Not overloading the dryer leads to quicker drying times.

If you have successfully avoided washing and dealing with your own clothes for the last eighteen years, the time to learn how to do this is before you go away to college. Ask whoever it is in your household who usually does the laundry to teach you the basic concepts. These concepts will be things like: don't put a red shirt in with white clothes unless you really like the color pink.

YOUR RESPONSIBILITY—EATING WELL

At college, no one is going to tell you to eat your vegetables. No one is going to limit the amount of soda or candy you eat while you're studying. You will likely have access to lots of food and you will want to eat. Sometimes you will want comfort food out of nervousness and stress. Sometimes you'll want food to be sociable and to hang out longer with your new friends. Sometimes you will be so busy that you'll find yourself just reaching for fast food for days at a time while you try to squeeze more hours out of each day.

Be careful. Remember that what you put into your mouth affects your whole body. It affects how well your brain functions, how much energy you have, and how strong your immune system is. Naturally, since you're putting a lot of new information into your brain, you will want

Reach for College!

it to be operating at peak performance. Since you are cramming a lot into each day, you will want to have lots of energy. And you will want your immune system to be warding off all the germs coming your way in your new living situation so you won't get sick.

A diet that's heavy on fast food, lots of soda, coffee or alcohol, junk food, and fatty foods will slowly wear you down. You will start to feel tired, slower, and can't think as well. You'll be susceptible to every germ that comes your way. So what can you do?

Remember that moderation is always best. You can eat the chips and soda, but eat limited amounts and balance that by also eating a salad. Does that thick piece of chocolate cake tempt you? Split it with your friend and save it until you've finished a healthy dinner of meat, vegetables and fruit.

Think back to the food groups you learned about in elementary school.
- Get protein every day—meat, chicken, fish, eggs.
- Get whole grains every day—cereal, whole wheat bread, rice.
- Get lots of vegetables every day—salads, peas, carrots, corn, broccoli, greens.
- Get lots of fruit every day—aim to eat fruit at every meal or eat fruit for snacks.
- Get calcium every day—milk, cheese, yogurt.
- Drink more water, milk and juices, less soda and coffee.

You'll also feel better if you eat "lighter".
- Don't eat until you're "stuffed" at every meal. Save that uncomfortable feeling for Thanksgiving.
- Go for potatoes, fish, and chicken that are boiled or baked, not battered and fried.
- Drink water with your meal, not soda.
- Eat fruit for dessert instead of a sweet.
- For snacking, substitute low-salt, no butter microwave popcorn instead of chips or nuts.

You will also feel better and function better if you eat meals at a regular, routine time every day. Your body gets accustomed to feeling hungry and full at certain times each day. If you skip meals and then stuff yourself at the next meal to catch up, your body's chemistry has a harder time regulating itself. So, it will make you feel weak and dizzy because of the skipped meal and make you feel sleepy and resistant to thinking after the big meal.

It's better to keep your body on an even balance by establishing a routine and sticking with it. When no one is telling you to come home for dinner or setting aside a particular time when everyone goes to eat in the cafeteria, like now at your high school, when you have complete nearly freedom to eat or not eat when you want, you have to responsible enough to take care of your body and establish a schedule that works.

YOUR RESPONSIBILITY—STAYING HEALTHY

Like eating well on a regular schedule, staying healthy is now your responsibility. No one likes being sick, and it's even worse at college when missed classes and missed days of reading can set you back very quickly. Further, it is no fun being laid up in bed when everyone

else is out socializing. And finally, you don't have anyone who will sympathize with you and take care of you the way you often had at home. So, it's really important to try to stay healthy.

How can you maintain your health? Again, remember what people have been telling you your whole life. The rules for healthy living boil down to these:
- Eat the right foods.
- Get enough sleep.
- Exercise.
- Wash your hands frequently (especially when you're around people who are sick.)
- "Play the tape to the end" and don't do stupid things that might put you in the emergency room.

Get enough sleep.
What about getting enough sleep? This is a tough one at college. First, everyone is on a different schedule. Your roommate might not have an 8:00 class and so she stays up until 3:00 AM studying with the light on. But if you do have an 8:00 class you probably want to go to bed before 3:00. Someone has set up bowling with plastic pins out in the hallway and with everyone cheering, it's impossible to sleep. Your best friend is having a crisis and needs to talk when you need to be snoozing.

Second, you might have so much to do that you feel you can't get more than a few hours a night. Third, you might be experiencing emotional issues, such as new love or missing people from home or being upset with someone on campus and thinking about all this is keeping you awake.

Yes, it's often hard to get enough sleep to stay healthy, but you've got to be aware of needing the rest and trying to get it in. Pay attention to what your body is telling you. If you are dragging, it's time to tape a 'please do not disturb' note on the door and take a nap. It's time to talk to your roommate about maybe studying in the lounge or in someone else's room. Call home to get a taste of what you're missing and to deal with your homesickness so you can sleep. In other words, **get active about solving your sleeping deficit.** It's important in your quest to stay healthy.

Exercise.
Don't forget to exercise. Exercise will physically tire you out so you'll drop off to sleep sooner and rest more deeply. Exercise also relieves stress and gets good chemicals racing around in your brain and body that also help to keep you healthy. Most campuses encourage students to exercise by providing free gym facilities where you can swim, work out, play a pick-up game of basketball, or run on the track. Fitting an hour or even a half hour of exercise into your day on a regular basis will ultimately give you more energy and keep your mind sharper.

Wash your hands.
This is a simple rule, but one that people often forget. Wash your hands before you eat. Wash your hands before you sit down to study. Wash your hands before you get in bed.

Remember that germs are what make you sick, and you pick up germs from your desk in class where other students have been sitting, from library books, from shaking hands, from any contact with surfaces where someone who is sick has sneezed or touched. So, if you touch these, then you've got the germs on your hands. Then if you eat or touch your face, you have transmitted the germs to yourself. If your immune system is in top shape and strong, you'll

probably be able to fight them off. But if you're run down or if the germs are strong enough, then you'll get sick. First-year students often get sick because they're exposed to new germs from literally all over the country, and they don't have immunity built up to them yet.

An ounce of prevention is literally worth a pound of cure in this case. Simply wash your hands frequently to rid yourself of germs. What could be easier? Is it too much work to get down to the bathroom all the time? Keep a bottle of antibacterial hand cleaner on your desk and use it.

Don't do stupid things.
Accidents of various kinds are the single largest cause of injury, illness and death in the 18-25 age range. One of the biggest reasons college students end up in the Health Center or Emergency Room is because they've done something stupid and risky. These include such things as:
- Getting in the car of a driver who has been drinking.
- Doing risky things to go along with the crowd.
- Drinking too much and getting alcohol poisoning or behaving in dangerous ways.
- Becoming pregnant or contracting a sexually transmitted disease.

While certain activities might start out as innocent and fun, it's important to "play the tape to the end" and see where things might lead. If you get seriously hurt or pregnant, this could effectively end your college days. Think ahead; be smart. Have the courage and discipline *not* to do stupid things that could have a lasting impact on your health and on your life.

YOUR RESPONSIBILITY—YOUR SAFETY

Just as no one is telling you when and how to eat or when to go to sleep or how to take care of yourself to stay healthy, now no one is telling you to "be careful" or to "be home at a reasonable hour" or to "avoid strangers" either. All of these safety phrases that you've been hearing all your life still apply; it's just that no one will be saying them to you as you go out the door at college. You have to tell them to yourself because you will be responsible for your own safety now.

Crimes happen on college campuses everyday. Sometimes the culprits are strangers who come onto campus. Other times the perpetrators are students or people you see every day. The important thing is to be as aware and as careful as you would be in any city neighborhood. Be alert and be smart. This means:
- Don't prop the door to the dorm open; use your key or student ID swipe card—for everyone's safety.
- Lock your own dorm room when you or your roommate are not going to be there.
- If you don't feel safe walking from place to place on the campus at night, ask a friend to accompany you or call for security to escort you.
- Follow all the procedures the college has set up for safety. They have been established for your benefit.

Reach for College!

Assignment #18

How do you think you'll do handling your new personal responsibilities?

Having read about several personal responsibilities that you will need to be handling on your own in the next few months, which of the ones below do you think will be the most challenging for you? Which ones will be the easiest?

- Keeping my living space and clothes clean.
- Eating a healthy diet on a regular schedule.
- Staying healthy by:
    1. Eating the right foods.
    2. Getting enough sleep.
    3. Exercising.
    4. Washing my hands frequently (especially when around people who are sick.)
    5. "Playing the tape to the end" and not doing risky things.
- Being careful to protect my personal safety.

1. For me, I think the most challenging of the ones above will be _____
_____
_____.

2. They will be challenging for me because _____
_____
_____.

3. For me, I think the easiest of the ones above will be _____
_____
_____.

4. They will be easy for me because _____
_____
_____.

5. What can I do now to "practice" and prepare myself for the ones above that I know will be challenging? _____
_____

6. When will you start this practice/preparation?_____

7. Who will be able to help you with this preparation? (This might be someone such as a family member—who might teach you good laundry techniques; or it might be a friend—who might be supportive as you both plan to exercise every day or to eat a healthier diet.)
_____

YOUR RESPONSIBILITY—MANAGING YOUR MONEY

Another area of life you will need to become responsible for is money management. This important aspect of adult life is often neglected in formal studies in high school, and chances are, your family has handled a big part of this up to now. Yet this is something that all young men and women should know about as they start off on a life of their own.

How have you managed money so far? If you've had a paying job while in high school, what's happened when you've gotten your paycheck? Maybe you gave some of the money to your family to help with bills or to buy groceries, and the rest you took and spent on those special shoes or that new outfit you'd been looking at.

If this has been your pattern, you are like most teenagers. Cash is hard to keep around. Somehow it just seems to disappear and then you're left anxiously waiting for the next check to buy the next thing you want. Maybe, you're waiting for your Mom to give you some money for the next thing you want to purchase. You probably haven't been thinking too much beyond that. That is the attitude of a teenager. As a young adult, now is the time to begin thinking more seriously and wisely about money.

MAKING A BUDGET AND LIVING WITHIN IT

This year you have been setting goals and making plans that you hope will propel you forward for the next few years toward the career goal you've chosen. You have probably learned that making a plan toward achieving your goal is a crucial part of actually reaching your dream.

A budget is a "money plan." It is a plan to help you toward whatever financial goal you choose. It is a way to get organized and disciplined about money so that money doesn't just disappear, but goes toward what you want it to. A budget can be made for a small amount of money or a large amount. The important thing is to have a goal and have a plan. A goal you might have for this summer is to save as much money from your summer job as you can so you will be able to have spending money at college in the fall or so you won't have to work in your first semester at college to give you the maximum amount of time to get adjusted to college life.

Here is an example of how a budget can help you toward your goals. Let's say that Mark has been working as a bagger at a local grocery store for several months. Mark likes getting the paycheck, but it still seems to him that he never has enough money. In addition, his mother has been saying that since he has a job, he should be helping with some household bills and not asking her for money anymore for things such as bus fare. She suggested he pay his own

monthly cell phone bill. He wants to help out, but whenever the phone bill is due, he comes up empty-handed, so his mother gets mad. How can a budget help Mark?

First, he needs to write down how much money he makes and what are his expenses, putting the most important ones first. Second, he should write down his goal or goals.

Weekly paycheck--$55.25   **Monthly amount--$221.00**

Goals: To pay phone bill
To pay for my own expenses and not bother Mom for money
To save for a stereo that costs $200

Expenses:

Phone bill—approximately	$35/month
Bus fare--$22.50/week	$90/month
Fast food on break from work--$15/week	$60/month
Clothes--$30/week	$120/month
Total	$305/month

It is easy to see why Mark comes up short every month, why he can't help with the phone bill, and why he's always asking his mother for money by looking at his list of expenses. By writing it all down, he can clearly see this. Something needs to happen. Either he needs to make more money or he needs to cut down on his expenses.

This is what Mark decides to do. He realizes that being lazy is costing him some money. He could get a monthly bus pass for $45, but he just never takes the time to do it. If he did that, he would save $45. He also recognizes that he doesn't have to eat fast food every day when he's at work. He just does it because the other guys go and hang out there on break. By cutting out the fast food every day except Saturday, when he really does need to eat, he can save $40. He likes to look sharp, but he also really wants a stereo. If he could cut his clothes shopping down to $75 per month or less, he could put the rest into saving for the stereo. Now Mark makes a budget that he will try to live within.

Expenses:

Phone bill	$35/month
Bus fare (monthly pass)	$45/month
Fast food on break from work--$5/week	$20/month
Clothes	$75/month
Total	$175/month
Saving for stereo	$46/month (after 4 months = $230)
Total	$221 (which equals his monthly earnings)

Mark also plans to start working longer hours once basketball season is over and he is no longer obligated to go to practices and games. The extra money could go into saving for the stereo, clothes, or for other spending money. Either way, Mark is glad he can see, in black and white, what he needs to do to achieve his goals.

...after Graduation

Once you're on your own or in college, budgeting will be very important because money will be tight. Everyone just starting out in the world has relatively little money. Employers pay less to recent high school graduates than to more experienced workers. And yet you, like everyone else have to pay for living expenses, transportation, etc.

Most students who are studying for a career after high school are poor. You will have little or no money coming in because you are devoting your time to school, but you have lots of expenses—everything from school supplies to computers to books, not to mention food, transportation, and other essentials.

It is crucial to learn how to be frugal (the way Mark realized he could save money by purchasing a monthly fare card and by cutting out the unneeded fast food). It's also crucial to learn how to budget your money so the things that *have* to be paid for actually *do* get paid for. With a budget you can see where it is possible to save some money that you might not be spending in the wisest way, and it gives you a plan to reach your financial goals.

Assignment #19

Create a budget for yourself.

Make up a budget for yourself. List your financial goals, your income and your expenses. Then, balance the budget, meaning that your income should at least cover your expenses and leave some left over to save, if possible.

1. Financial goals (list most important ones first):

   _____

   _____

2. Total Income: _____

3. Expenses:

   _____   _____

   _____   _____

   _____   _____

4. Total Expenses: _____

5. Does your income equal or surpass your expenses? _____

6. Where are some places that you can save money?

_____

_____

7. Construct a balanced budget that will help you reach your financial goals.
(Remember a "balanced budget" means that your income will equal or surpass your expenses.)

_____

_____

_____

_____

_____

_____

_____

_____

Total Income = _____   Total Expenses = _____

8. Will this budget plan help you to reach your financial goals? _____

LEARN ABOUT BANK ACCOUNTS—CHECKING AND SAVINGS

Checking Accounts

One of the easiest and most responsible things you can do is to become acquainted with banks and what they offer. Two of the most basic services banks offer are checking and savings accounts. You should know about each of these and how they work.

A checking account is a service whereby you put money into a special account that has a number just for you. If you have a checking account at a bank, then you can cash your checks for free, unlike at the corner grocery store or check cashing service, where they charge a certain percentage. The money you put into the account is kept safely there until you take it out. But you can get to it whenever you want. You can take it out a couple of ways. You can write a check, or you can use an ATM card.

Just as your employer gave you a check for the amount of money he or she owed you, if you owe money to someone (for a phone bill, etc.), you can give or mail them a check for the amount you owe. This is more convenient and safer than carrying around cash. You can mail a check, but you should never mail cash.

You just have to be sure that you have enough money in your account to cover the check. In other words you can't write a check for more money than you have in your account. If you do, the bank charges you about $35 for overdrawing your account.

If you handle your checking account responsibly, this goes on a record called your credit report which will help you financially in the future. (More about this later.)

There are several advantages and a few disadvantages of having a checking account:

Advantages:	**Disadvantages:**
You can cash checks for free.	Depending on what type of account you open, there can be a monthly fee ($4 or more) to maintain a checking account. However, banks often have account-types for students that charge no monthly fee.
You can write checks to pay for things and send them in mail.	The checks themselves cost about $12 for 200 checks.
Checks are safer and more convenient than cash.	You have to be sure not to overdraw your account.
Responsible use of a checking account leads to a good credit rating.	Irresponsible use of a checking account leads to a bad credit rating.

Savings Accounts

A savings account, like a checking account, is a service whereby you put money into a bank and the bank keeps it safe in a special account just for you. For a savings account, the bank pays you a certain amount of interest (usually 2-3%) on the money you have in the account.

A savings account is a very good idea, so you have some money set aside in case of emergencies or if you are saving up for a big purchase. You know it is safe, and your money grows because the bank pays you interest. No one can get to it except you, and you have to think twice before spending it, because you have to go to the bank and fill out a withdrawal slip in order to take the money out. But it requires a great deal of discipline to put the money in and leave it.

Reach for College!

VOCABULARY OF BANKING

Bankers use special vocabulary, which is not difficult to learn. But you should know some of it before you go to the bank to open an account, so you will know what they are talking about.

Deposit/Credit—Any time you put money into your account you are making a deposit. The bank credits (adds to) your account with that amount.

Endorse—Any time you have a check that you want to cash or deposit, you must endorse the back of it. This means you sign your name the same way it appears on the front of the check. (If the check is made payable to you using your middle initial, for example, then you should sign the back using your middle initial too.) If you have an account at the bank, you will also write your account number on the back of the check.

Withdrawal/Debit—Any time you take money out of your account you make a withdrawal. The bank debits (subtracts from) your account by that amount.

Interest-bearing—Savings accounts and some checking accounts pay interest of 2-5% (depending on current rates) on the money you have in the account. Therefore, it is called an interest-bearing account. Generally, to get interest on a checking account, you have to agree to always keep a certain sum of money in the account.

Passbook—If you open a savings account, the bank may give you a passbook, which is a little book in which you can keep an accounting of how much you have in your savings account and in which you can keep a record of what you deposit and what you withdraw.

Service charge—Some banks charge small monthly fees on checking accounts, called service charges or fees, for various things the bank does for you. When you go to open an account tell them that you want an account with the lowest or no service charges. They will probably tell you about student accounts or other kinds of accounts wherein, if you don't write many checks per month, there is a very low or no service charge. Banks have many different kinds of accounts, so be sure to ask about what their different kinds of accounts offer, and choose the one that seems to fit your needs best.

Statement—At the end of each month you will get a statement from the bank that lists all the deposits, withdrawals and checks you wrote—all the activity on your account that month. It will also give you an ending balance of how much money you had in your account at the time the statement was dated.

Balance your account—In order to make sure you always have enough money in the bank, it is necessary to balance your account—to add up all the withdrawals and the checks you have written and to make sure you have deposited enough money to balance with what you've taken out. A good time to do this is when you get your monthly statement. Go through what you wrote down in your account register (see below) and reconcile that with what the bank says you did with your account. In other words, make sure your records match the bank's records listed on

Reach for College!

your statement. Then, make sure your account balances, that means your final totals equal the bank's totals.

Account register—This is a small booklet the size of your checks in which you write down all your deposits, withdrawals and checks, so you can keep a running balance of how much money you have in your account at any time. Be sure to write in your account register *every time* you write a check, use your ATM/check card, or make a withdrawal.

Outstanding checks—When you get your account statement at the end of each month, there are likely to be checks you have written that didn't come into the bank before the statement was mailed. These are called outstanding checks. When you balance your account by checking it with your statement, it is important to remember to include the outstanding checks.

ATM—Automatic Teller Machine. You can do banking, such as withdrawing and depositing money, at ATM machines. You have to have a bank issued card, like a credit card, to use one. ATM cards are free. You just have to ask to see if one comes with the type of account you are getting.

Electronic withdrawals—Withdrawals that you do with your ATM card at an ATM or at a grocery store, for instance, are called electronic withdrawals. It is important to remember to write down your electronic withdrawals just as you do your checks, so you don't forget you made the withdrawal and overdraw your account. (You should also be aware that if you use an ATM that is different from your bank's ATM, you are usually charged a fee of $2.00 or more. You can avoid getting charged, generally, if you use your own bank's ATMs.)

Overdraft—Overdrawing your account means that you wrote a check or made an electronic withdrawal for more money than you had in your account. This causes an overdraft, which the bank penalizes you for by charging you a hefty service charge, usually about $35 per overdraft. So always be careful to be aware of your balance, and don't take out more money than you have. You don't want to lose $35 of your hard-earned money just for being careless.

BANKING FORMS

Just as there is a specialized vocabulary for banking, bankers also use specialized forms that are similar at all banks. It is a good idea to be familiar with these forms, what they are for and when to use each one.

Making a Deposit—You can deposit cash or checks into a checking account. But either way, you have to use a deposit slip. Deposit slips for your specific account are at the back of each of your books of checks. They already have your account number and name printed on them.

They usually ask for the date and the amount you are depositing. Besides filling in this information, you must endorse the back of the check, if it is a check you are depositing, and write your account number on the back of the check. As a safety measure, it's a good idea to also write, "Deposit only." This way, if you drop the endorsed check or otherwise lose it, no one can just go and get it cashed, because it says it can only be deposited in the account whose number is listed right there.

Reach for College!

Check-writing—To write a check, you fill in the blanks on the check itself. These blanks are:
- **Date**—the date you are writing the check

- **Pay to the order of**—who you are writing the check to, such as Verizon, or Macy's Department Store, or Giant grocery store.

- **$**--at the end of the line of "Pay to the order of", there is a dollar sign and a short line or box. There you write the amount of the check using numbers.

- **Amount written out in words**—on the line below "Pay to the order of" write out the amount of the check in words, such as "One hundred seventeen and 40/100 dollars". The amount in cents is often written in a fraction on the same line. So 40 cents is written 40/100.

- **Your signature**—on the bottom line on the right, sign your name.

- **For/Memo**—on the bottom line on the left you can write what this check is for if you want to or you don't have to. It is the only thing on a check that is not required. You might say, for example, repair of roller blades, or if you are paying a bill, you might write your account number with that store or company. If it is a phone bill, for example, you would write your phone number on that line, so clerks receiving these checks at the phone company will be sure to credit the right account with having paid the bill.

Withdrawing cash—To withdraw money in cash from your checking account, all you do is write a check. On the line "Pay to the order of" you write "Cash" or your own name. Then you fill out everything else on the check as usual. Write in how much cash you want. Endorse it on the back just like you would any other check, and present it to the teller. They will take the check and give you cash.

Assignment #20

Practice using banking terms and forms.

Use the words below to fill in the blanks of the following story. (Some of the words can be used more than once.)

check register	service charge	endorse
electronic withdrawal	statement	balance
deposit	interest bearing	overdraw
withdrawal/debit		

Tiffany decided to open a checking account at the bank near her school. Her employer had just given her a check for $252 that included all the overtime hours she had worked during the Christmas season. She took her photo ID, the check, and her social security card to the bank. She knew she had to wait for one of the bank employees who sit at a desk rather than one of the tellers behind the counter in order to open an account. She signed in on the sheet and sat down

...after Graduation   95

to wait for a customer service manager. Shortly, a man in a suit called her name and asked her how he could help her. Tiffany said she wanted to open a checking account. He showed Tiffany to his desk and asked her to sit down.

He explained about the different types of checking accounts they offered and suggested that the one for students might be best for her because there was no _____ if she wrote no more than ten checks per month. Tiffany agreed. Then he asked for her ID and her social security card, and he put her name into the computer.

As he was setting up her account on the computer, he asked her how much money she intended to _____ to open her account. Tiffany told him $252 and she showed him her check. He said that was fine and asked her to _____ the check on the back. Then he took her check and the new account information to one of the tellers, who officially put the money into the new account.

While he was gone, Tiffany started to think about some questions she had about her new account. So when he came back she asked, "Is it possible to get an ATM card with this account?"

"Yes," he said, if you fill out this card, one will come to you in the mail. Then you can make an _____ at any ATM machine. As long as you do that at one of our bank's machines, there is no service fee, but if you do it at another bank's machine, it will give you the money, but there will be a $2.00 charge deducted. If you do that, you should be sure to make note of that charge in your _____ so you won't accidentally _____ the account. A $35 charge is a painful lesson to learn for not writing all withdrawals and all service charges into your account register. Of course, they will show up on your monthly _____. And then you can accurately _____ your account. But I just caution our teenage customers, not to just use that ATM card without thinking."

The other question Tiffany had was about a savings account. "If I were to open a savings account, is there any sort of minimum balance I'd have to maintain in it in order to get interest?"

"No," he responded. "All of our savings accounts are _____. Did you want to open a savings account today too?"

"No thank you," Tiffany responded. "I have to make some more money first."

Then he showed her a book with many different kinds of checks that she could choose from. Some had clouds, landscape scenes, or animals on them, but those cost more. She decided on getting just the basic checks. He told her the cost of the checks ($12) would be automatically deducted from her account and the checks would be sent to her in the mail.

So, as he finished the paperwork for her new account and got her a few temporary checks, she wrote the first _____ in her account register--$12 for checks. That came out of the $252 she had _____, so her _____ now was $240.

Reach for College!

Tiffany left the bank feeling grown-up and responsible. She was going to be good at this, she could just tell.

Banking Forms

Practice using the banking forms below.

By the time Tiffany got her next paycheck for $175, her checks and a couple of bills had arrived. Help Tiffany do all the banking she needs to do.

She needs to deposit her check for $175.

She needs to pay three bills:
    Macy's $43.24
    Bell Atlantic $32.75
    BMG Music Club $22.49

She wants to get $50 in cash from her account to go shopping for a birthday gift for her brother.

...after Graduation

Deposit Slip

DEPOSIT TICKET

Tiffany Waldrop
36 Cedars Drive
City, State

DATE _____

DEPOSIT MIGHT NOT BE AVAILABLE FOR IMMEDIATE WITHDRAWAL

_____
SIGN HERE IF CASH RECEIVED

CASH _____
CHECKS _____
_____
_____

SUBTOTAL
LESS CASH _____
TOTAL DEPOSIT _____

Bank

540638   00326759036

Check Register

Check Number	Date	Transaction Description	Amount of Deposit	Amount of Withdrawal/Payment	Fee (if any)	Balance

Reach for College!

Checks

```
Tiffany Waldrop                                              1481
36 Cedars Drive
City, State
Phone                                          Date _____

Pay to the order of _____  $ _____

_____ Dollars

     Bank

For _____   _____

   540638      00326759036
```

```
Tiffany Waldrop                                              1482
36 Cedars Drive
City, State
Phone                                          Date _____

Pay to the order of _____  $ _____

_____ Dollars

     Bank

For _____   _____

   540638      00326759036
```

```
Tiffany Waldrop                                              1483
36 Cedars Drive
City, State
Phone                                          Date _____

Pay to the order of _____  $ _____

_____ Dollars

     Bank

For _____   _____

   540638      00326759036
```

...*after Graduation*

```
Tiffany Waldrop                                      1484
36 Cedars Drive
City, State
Phone                                       Date _____

Pay to the order of _____  $ _____

_____ Dollars

     Bank
For _____    _____

     540638      00326759036
```

CREDIT CARDS

Credit cards and how they work is another area you should be familiar with as you start to take control of your own financial affairs. Credit cards are everywhere. You can get credit cards from department stores, gas stations, furniture stores, and large national companies such as VISA, MasterCard, Discover or American Express. In fact, when you turn eighteen, you will probably be actively solicited to open credit card accounts. You might get offers in the mail, or when you buy something at a department store. They might ask you if you'd like to put it on their charge account and most likely will offer you 10% off of that purchase, if you fill out an application for their credit card right then and there.

It's easy to buy things using a credit card. Hey, you don't have to pay anything, right? You just hand them the plastic and walk out with your purchase. What could be better? **It is very tempting to open credit card accounts all over the place and start charging. In fact, that is what a lot of teenagers do. They get caught in a trap.**

What you must realize is that buying something with a credit card is actually borrowing money. The credit card company, essentially, gives you a loan. They pay the store for whatever it is you buy, and then you owe the credit card company the money, plus interest. Often the interest rate is very high. If you read the tiny, scrunched together fine print at the bottom of the credit card application, it will say that you will pay usually between 18%-21% interest on the money you have "borrowed." That means if you buy an outfit for $100. You will actually be paying $115-$121 for it if you pay it off quickly. If you let it go and don't pay off the bill quickly, that outfit might cost you a great deal more. This is something to consider seriously when you start charging. It's so easy to use a credit card that you can get in way over your head before you even know what has happened.

However, **credit cards are handy, and there *is* a way to beat the system. If you pay off the total bill each month, by the due date, there is no interest charged at all.** In other words, if you pay the total amount you owe by the date due, you never will pay any extra. That

Reach for College!

means being very disciplined, not going overboard with your purchases, keeping track of what you've bought, and having the money to be able to pay the bill when it comes in the mail. Otherwise, you will be paying interest and the interest keeps getting added to the bill, until eventually you are being charged interest on the interest. Be careful. Be responsible with credit cards.

Assignment #21

Get familiar (but not in over your head) with credit cards.

Here is a typical credit card bill. Answer the questions below about this bill.

Fleet — Visa Gold Statement
Account no. xxxx-0000-xxxx-0000

Previous balance	$94.18
Payments and credits	− 94.18
Purchases and other charges	+ 195.93
Cash advances	+ 0.00
FINANCE CHARGES	+ 0.00
New balance	$195.93

Statement closing date	10/25/00
Minimum payment	$13.00
Payment due date	11/21/00
Days in billing cycle	29

Credit Line

Total credit line	$8,800
Cash advance credit line	$4,400
Credit available	$8,605
Available portion for cash advance	$4,400

Account Information

Transactions

Tran Date	Posting Date	Reference Number	Description	Amount
09/26	09/27	2422638LYAFQF9DBF	SAMS RECORDS AND TAPES	52.87
09/28	09/27	2430775LY01 8841 PG	US POST OFFICE	18.70
10/04	10/04	2438775M6018896F4	BORDERS BOOKS	17.50
10/04	10/04	741 2459M62SL364X4	PAYMENT - THANK YOU	94.18
10/07	10/07	2439907MA5F378SEW	OFFICE MAX	32.09
10/08	10/08	2422638MAMFRH1DWS	MACY'S	44.90
10/13	10/13	2144571MF7JD41XHA	KROGER	14.88
10/13	10/13	2404571MF7JD41XKX	HALLMARK	14.99

Finance Charge Summary

Rate Category	Nominal ANNUAL PERCENTAGE RATE	Daily Periodic Rate	Average Daily Balance	FINANCE CHARGE Periodic	Transaction Fee
Purchases	19.97%	.05470%	0.00	0.00	
Advances	21.97%	.08018%	0.00	0.00	
ANNUAL PERCENTAGE RATE	Purchases	19.97%	Advances	21.97%	

Reach for College!

...after Graduation

1. What is the new balance on this credit card? _____

2. How much does this person have to pay this month in order to avoid paying any finance charges? _____

3. When is this bill due (which means payment must be in the hands of the credit card company by this date)? _____

4. What is the minimum payment that must be made? _____

5. How much was the bill last month? _____

6. How much was paid? _____

7. Did the person accrue any finance charges? _____

8. How much money did the person spend at the bookstore this month? _____

9. How much money did the person spend at Macy's this month? _____

10. How much is the Annual Percentage Rate on purchases for this card? _____

11. How much is the credit line on this card? _____

12. What is "credit line"? _____

13. How much credit is available to this person at this time? _____

14. What is a "cash advance" _____
_____

15. How much of a cash advance would this person be able to get at this time? _____

16. Do you think you could be a responsible user of a credit card? _____

BUYING A CAR—GETTING A LOAN

There is nothing like having a car to make you feel truly independent: to be able to come and go as you please, to be able to drive to places that are hard to reach by public transportation, to be able to get out of town when you feel like it is a great feeling. And you probably feel like you are ready for that kind of freedom now.

Maybe you've been able to borrow a car from your parents, an aunt or uncle, and use it occasionally, but what you would really like is a car of your own. How does someone go about buying a car?

Reach for College!

Unless you have been saving for a long time or have recently come into a lot of money, you probably don't have the several thousand dollars needed to buy an inexpensive used car. Or maybe you have your heart set on something a little more upscale and new. Either way, you like most people, will need to borrow money, take out a loan, in order to buy a car. What does this entail?

First, you might look in the newspaper in the car advertising section and see if there are certain banks that are advertising special car loans. You could call or visit them. Car dealerships will help you get a loan through their financing departments. You could go to your own bank and ask about their car loans. They will tell you:
- What you need to do in order to qualify for a loan.
- How much money they want you to bring as a down payment on the car.
- How much they charge in interest.

What you need to do to qualify for a loan

Before banks will lend you money they want to make sure that you will pay them back. So, banks will want to know some things about you. These are:
1. What kind of job do you have and how much does it pay? (Does it pay enough for you to be able to afford a car?)
2. How long have you been working at this job? (Are you reliable and is it likely that you will stick with this job or a similar one long enough to pay back the loan?)
3. What other bills do you have? (When all these other bills are added up is there still enough money in your paycheck to make the monthly payments for the loan?)
4. What is your credit history? (What else have you borrowed money for in the past and how well did you pay that back? Did you make all the payments on time?)

The lender will have you fill out an application, which asks many of the questions above. It usually takes several days for them to process your application and part of what they do is check your credit report.

Credit Reports

A credit report is a record of your credit history—kind of report card of how well you have paid your bills in the past. This report is kept by several credit history companies in the country. These companies are alerted if you don't pay your credit card bills on time, if you skip out of an apartment without paying the rent, or if you don't pay your phone bills on time, for instance. Similarly, they keep track of times when you owed money for something and you paid it back to a bank or a store. They note whether your payments were on time or not. You can have a good credit report or a bad credit report. Obviously, if your credit report is good, you will have a better chance of getting a car loan than if your credit report is bad.

Co-signers

If this is the first loan you are applying for and you have never really been responsible for paying bills before, you probably don't have a credit history at all. In that case, the bank will ask you to have a co-signer. A co-signer is someone who is willing to sign onto the loan with you and who will guarantee the bank that they will pay the loan even if for some reason, you don't.

This way the bank is protected, and you can begin getting a credit history of your own. This co-signer, of course, has to have a good credit history and be willing to help you out in this way.

Down payment

After you fill out the application and get a co-signer, if necessary, the bank will want to know how much money you are putting "down." This means how much of a down payment are you making. Usually, when buying a car, you have to bring some money to the deal, and quite often at least 10%-20% is required.

Length of loan

The bank will also want to know how long you want to take to pay back the loan—the "term" of the loan. You can choose a variety of lengths of time to pay off a loan— between one to five years, usually depending on the size of the loan. (Car loans are often stated in months, and a 48-month loan, for example, will take you four years to pay off.) If you choose to pay the loan off quickly, then each monthly payment will be larger. If you choose to pay it off over several years, then your payments will be smaller, but you will end up paying more interest. It is your choice.

Interest

Interest is the fee you are charged for borrowing the money. This fee is figured as a percentage of the amount you borrow. The amount of this fee varies according to how much banks and the government are charging each other for borrowing money and often on the quality of your credit history. A better credit history usually gets you a better interest rate. But generally, you can count on a car loan interest rate as being between 7%-14%. This means, if you borrow $1000 and the interest rate is 10%, you will end up paying $1100 altogether.

Monthly payments

If you decide to borrow $1000 at an interest rate of 10% for a one-year period, you figure your monthly payments this way.

$$\$1000 + \$100 \text{ (interest)} = \$1100$$

$$1 \text{ year} = 12 \text{ months}$$

$$\$1100 \text{ divided by } 12 = \$91.66$$

You will have to pay $91.66 every month for one year to pay off your loan.

Other things to keep in mind about buying a car

When buying a car, it is important to keep in mind that there are many other expenses that you might not think about right away, but that will definitely eat into any budget. These are:
- **Sales tax, license, tags, title, registration**: Every state requires you to register your vehicle and get license plates to go on the car. The process and the cost for this varies from state to state, but it is worth looking into before you go to purchase a car. Usually, you must pay a sales tax on the car before they issue the tags and registration. This sales tax (5%-9% depending on your state) is quite a chunk of money. Sometimes, people roll

this into their loan; in other words, they ask for the amount of the sales tax to be part of the loan amount. So, if the car costs $5000 and the sales tax is 6%, which equals $300, they might ask for a loan of $5300.
- **Insurance is also required.** Depending on your age, the age of the car, the kind of car, and your driving record, insurance can cost between $400-$2000 per year.
- **Maintenance**, such as oil changes, new tires, and repairs can be quite costly.
- **Gas.**
- **Parking**—Do you a have free, safe place to park your car, or will you be charged for parking at home, at school or at work?

Finishing the deal

When your loan application is approved, you (and your co-signer, if you have one) will go back to the bank to sign the loan agreement. The loan agreement is usually several pages long and explains all the details of the contract. It explains:
1. How much the principal is (the actual amount of money you are borrowing).
2. What the interest rate is.
3. Altogether how much you must pay each month.
4. When you must make your monthly payment.
5. Late charge amounts if you do not make the payment on time.
6. How much your down payment is.

Once you sign the loan agreement, the bank will give you a check for the amount of the principal and the loan is complete.

Assignment #22

Application for a Loan

Fill out the application below as if you were applying for a car loan.

Bank
Credit Application

1. Tell us about your request. The purpose of loan is to: (Circle one)

Purchase Auto   Refinance Auto
Purchase, refinance, or improve home
Purchase Boat   Refinance Boat
Pay Educational Expenses
Consolidate Debts
Other

Amount requested $ _____

2. Tell us about yourself.
Name (First, Middle Initial, Last) _____
Social Security Number _____
Date of Birth _____

...after Graduation

Residential Status: Live with Parents/Relatives   Homeowner   Rent   Other

Current Address: Street _____
City _____ State _____   Zip _____
Date Moved to Address _____
Home Phone Number _____
Complete if moved to current address less than two years ago.
Previous Address: Street _____ City _____
State _____ Zip _____
Date Moved to Previous Address _____

Mortgage Holder or Landlord _____
Mortgage or Rent Payment (Per month) _____
Mortgage Balance (if homeowner) _____
Estimated Value of Home _____
Nearest Relative Not Living with You _____
Relationship to You _____   Home Phone Number _____

Current Employment Information:
Employer Name _____
Current Position/Title _____
Date Started with Current Employer _____
Number of Years in Current Profession _____
Work Phone Number _____
Gross (Before Tax) Income Sources:
Salary $ _____   How Often? _____
Bonus $ _____   How Often? _____
Commission $ _____   How Often? _____
(If Self-Employed attach 2 years tax returns)
Other Sources $ _____   How Often? _____
Specify Sources

Notice: Alimony, child support, or separate maintenance need not be revealed if you do not want it considered as a basis for repaying this obligation.

3. Tell us about the co-applicant, if this is a joint application.
Co-Applicant Name (First, Middle Initial, Last) _____
Social Security Number _____
Date of Birth _____

Residential Status: Live with Parents/Relatives   Homeowner   Rent   Other

Current Address: Street _____
City _____ State _____   Zip _____
Date Moved to Address _____
Home Phone Number _____
Complete if moved to current address less than two years ago.
Previous Address: Street _____ City _____
State _____ Zip _____
Date Moved to Previous Address _____

Mortgage Holder or Landlord _____
Mortgage or Rent Payment (Per month) _____
Mortgage Balance (if homeowner) _____
Estimated Value of Home _____
Nearest Relative Not Living with You _____

Reach for College!

Relationship to You _____ Home Phone Number _____

Current Employment Information:
Employer Name _____
Current Position/Title _____
Date Started with Current Employer _____
Number of Years in Current Profession _____
Work Phone Number _____
Gross (Before Tax) Income Sources:
Salary $ _____ How Often? _____
Bonus $ _____ How Often? _____
Commission $ _____ How Often? _____
(If Self-Employed attach 2 years tax returns)
Other Sources $ _____ How Often? _____
Specify Sources

Notice: Alimony, child support, or separate maintenance need not be revealed if you do not want it considered as a basis for repaying this obligation.

4. **Tell us about your bank accounts.** Also include those of the co-applicant, if this is a joint application. (Attach an additional sheet if necessary).
Bank Name _____
Checking Account # _____ Current balance $ _____
Savings Account # _____ Current balance $ _____
CD, IRA, or Other _____ Current amount $ _____

5. **Tell us about your debts.** Also include those of the co-applicant, if this is a joint application. (Attach an additional sheet if necessary)

Name of Company You Owe	Type of Debt You Owe (Credit Card, Loan, Mortgage, etc.)	Current Balance Outstanding	Minimum Monthly Payment

6. My/Our Total Assets $ _____ minus Total Debts $ _____ equals Net Worth $ _____

7. **Tell us about the Stocks, Bonds, Mutual Funds, Savings, or CD you are offering as collateral, if applicable.**

Stock, Bond or Mutual Fund Name _____
Number of Stock _____ Shares Value per Share of Stock _____
Value of Mutual Funds _____ Face Value of Bonds _____
CUSIP Numbers _____

8. **Tell us about your marital status IF your credit request will be secured.**
Applicant is: Married   Unmarried   Separated
Co-Applicant is: Married   Unmarried   Separated

Federal law requires that we request the following information for the types of credit requests described above in order to monitor the lender's compliance with equal credit opportunity, fair housing, and home mortgage disclosure laws. The gathering of this information will have no bearing on our lending decision. You are not required to furnish this information, but are encouraged to do so. The law provides that a lender may not discriminate on the basis of this information, or on whether you choose to furnish it.

Reach for College!

...after Graduation

However, if you choose not to furnish the information and you have made this application in person, under Federal regulations the lender is required to note race or national origin and sex on the basis of visual observation or surname. **If your loan request is for a purpose described above, you are requested to provide this information.**
Race or National Origin:

American Indian, Alaskan Native (1) Asian, Pacific Islander (2) Black (3) Hispanic (4)

White (6) Other (specify) (6)

Gender: Male   Female

I want to make my payments automatically from (please attach a deposit slip or voided check for the account to be drafted):
    my checking account # _____ at _____ Bank or my
    savings account # _____ at _____ Bank

9. Signature

Everything that I (we) have stated in this application is correct to the best of my (our) knowledge. I (we) understand that you will retain this application whether or not it is approved. You are authorized to check my (our) credit and employment history and to answer questions about your credit experience with me (us). You are also authorized to furnish to Bank of America Corporation or any of its subsidiaries information which I (we) have provided to you and information regarding my (our) accounts. If this is an application for a Personal CreditLine (unsecured line of credit), then I (we) acknowledge receipt of and agree to the terms of the Personal CreditLine Agreement and Disclosure.

Applicant's Signature   Date

Co-Applicant's Signature (if applicable)   Date

STUDENT LOANS TO FINANCE HIGHER EDUCATION

    Another kind of loan that you might be looking at in the near future is a student loan to pay for college. Quite often when you meet with the financial aid officer at your college to get everything lined up before you start school in the fall, the officer will show you a list of items that go into making up your "financial aid package." Taken all together, this package should add up to the total amount that you owe the school in order to pay for your first year. Here is a typical financial aid package:

Total amount owed to college for freshman year =	$10,000
Financial aid package	
Pell grant	$3000
Supplemental Educational Opportunity Grant	$1000
Scholarship	$1000
Work study	$2000
Loan	<u>$3000</u>
Total	$10,000

    You might think everything looks okay until you get to the last item and see that it is a loan, and then you start to worry. You think, "If I need to have a $3000 loan for all four years that I'm here, I'm going to leave school with $12,000 in debt, plus all the interest. How am I ever going to pay all that back? Maybe I shouldn't go to college, because I don't want all that debt to start with in life."

Reach for College!

First, you must remember that your earning power for the rest of your life with a college degree will be so much more than your earning power without a degree, that even with debt, you will be better off going to college. Second, student loans are different in several respects from other kinds of loans. Student loans:
- Have very low interest rates, usually about 2%-3%. That means for a loan of $3000, the interest for a year is only $90.
- You do not have to pay anything on your loan until you graduate or leave school.
- There are very easy, long-term pay-off plans that allow you to pay back student loans and not cramp your living style. Typical repayment plans for student loans average $50-$150 per month.

So, do not be too worried if the financial aid officer of your college signs you up for a student loan. Think of it as an investment in your future that you don't have to pay for until the future.

UNDERSTAND THE VALUE OF KEEPING A GOOD CREDIT REPORT

The purpose of this part of the chapter has been to inform you about some of the financial opportunities and responsibilities that come with adulthood. It is important to budget your money carefully because there are grave consequences for not dealing with your finances responsibly. Remember to:
- Have a clear picture of exactly how much money you have coming in.
- Write down/keep track of exactly how much money you are spending.
- Don't spend more than you have.
- Set clear financial goals for yourself and make a budget in order to reach your goals.
- If you acquire a credit card, try to pay off the balance as quickly as possible to avoid hefty finance charges.
- Pay all bills on time to avoid late charges.
- Don't overdraw your bank account, thereby incurring $35 overdraft fees.
- If you take out a loan for something—for a car or for educational expenses—pay back every penny and do it on time.

If you follow all these rules, you will be rewarded with having a good credit report. A good credit report is essentially a key that will easily unlock future financial doors. If you need a loan in the future to start a business, to buy a car, or to buy a home, you will be able to get the money and at a cheaper interest rate than if you have a bad credit report.

If you have a bad credit report, banks and other lenders are unlikely to lend you money. Landlords will not want to rent apartments to you or if they do, they will charge you large sums of money as a deposit, and it is hard to come up with that kind of cash. Credit card companies will not give you a credit card. All of these doors and many others will be locked to you.

You have probably seen advertisements about companies who will help you get around your bad credit. Yes, they might loan money to you or help you consolidate your debts. But the interest rate will be so high that you will be kept poor just paying all the extra interest. It will be

...after Graduation

hard to keep ahead of your bills.

It is much better, since you are starting out fresh and clean now, to do things right from the beginning. Think carefully about how you spend your money, don't exceed what you have, and you will be setting excellent habits that will give you a more secure financial future.

Assignment #23

Help Trisha get her financial life in order so she'll be able to retain good credit.

Trisha is about to move into her first apartment by herself. She is enrolled as a freshman at the local college and is working part-time. She also has a scholarship that covers part of her living expenses, and she has saved some money from her summer job. But she is overwhelmed by all the new financial responsibilities. And she is disorganized. She wants to get a small business loan to start a business when she graduates, so she wants to make sure her credit report is squeaky clean four years from now.

Help her get her life in order by sorting through all her bills and financial obligations, her assets, and make up a monthly budget for her with a time schedule for when certain bills must be paid. Help her balance her budget.

Trisha has been so busy getting started at school and moving into her studio apartment that she hasn't paid attention to any of the financial stuff. As things came in the mail or when she deposited a check in her checking account, she just threw everything into a shoe box on her bedside table.

1. Go through the shoe box and first sort things into columns below of "assets" (money she has) and "liabilities" (money she owes.)

Going from top to bottom in the shoe box:

Deposit receipt from bank—deposit from her job (every two weeks On 1st and 15th of month)	$78.25
Phone bill (due on 7th of each month)	$36.33
Rent (due on 1st of each month)	$375.00
Scholarship for living expenses (check comes on 1st of each month)	$700.00
Electric and heat bill (due on 20th of each month)	$ 55.00
Kroger receipt (groceries every week)	$ 66.00
Public transportation pass receipt (buy on 3rd of each month)	$ 45.00
Discover card bill (varies from $25-$75 per month—for items at drug store, clothes, CD's, etc.—due on 21st of each month)	$ 38.42
Lab fee at school ($75 per semester—due at beginning of semester)	$ 75.00
School supplies—notebooks, paper and ink cartridge for printer (will probably last for one semester)	$ 53.84
Savings account passbook balance (from summer job)	$1245.00
Checking account statement—balance	$ 61.25
Advertisement for a $175 TV at Best Buy (would love to get a TV)	$175.00
Need to get a winter coat—it's getting cold, old coat is now too small	$150.00

Reach for College!

Receipts for lunches at school—fast food ($5/day=$25/week) $25.00

Assets:

Receives every month:

On the 1st of the month   On the 15th of the month   In accounts now:

_____

_____

_____

_____

_____

Total assets each month_____   Assets in bank _____

Liabilities:

Owes every month: Every week: Beginning
1st of the month   15th of the month   of semester

_____

_____

_____

_____

Total liabilities:
1st _____   15th _____   Weekly _____   Semester _____

Total liabilities each month _____
(Don't forget to multiply her weekly costs times 4 to add to the monthly costs.)

Total liability at beginning of semester_____

Needs:

_____

_____

_____

Make up a Budget for Trisha:

Financial Goals:

_____

...after Graduation _____ 111
_____

Deposit:

On 1st of month: on 15th of month:
_____
_____

Total for 1st-15th _____   Total for 15th-31st _____

Withdraw money out of her savings account to deposit in her checking account to make up difference between monthly assets and liabilities. (She intends to work and save again next summer.)

How much each month? _____   Deposit when? _____

Monthly Budget:

Pay bill on 1st of month   Pay bill on 15th of month

_____

_____

_____

_____

$ for groceries and lunches each week = _____ x 2 weeks = _____ (Add this amount to each total below.)

Total payments for 1st two weeks of month = _____

Total payments for 2nd two weeks of month = _____

1. Does the total for checks Trisha will be writing to pay bills on the 1st plus the cash she will withdraw to pay for groceries and lunches for two weeks equal the amount of money she will have in the bank on the 1st of the month? _____

2. Does the total for checks Trisha will be writing to pay bills on the 15th plus the cash she will withdraw to pay for groceries and lunches for two weeks equal the amount of money she will have in the bank on the 15th of the month? _____

3. Will Trisha have enough money in her savings account to pay for the second semester lab fees and school supplies she will need? _____

4. Does she have money left over to put toward buying a coat or a TV? _____

Reach for College!

5. Which one should she buy first? _____ Why?

_____

_____

6. Will Trisha reach her financial goals by using this budget? _____

7. What recommendations do you have for Trisha about how she should spend her money or ways to save money to help her reach her financial goals?

_____

_____

_____

_____

"At first financial planning may seem a bit overwhelming, but if you think of it as a guide to a better life you may just find yourself creating your own financial treasure map."
~Gracian Mack

Chapter Eight

"So I set a goal of becoming a starter on the varsity. That's what I focused on all summer. When I worked on my game, that's what I thought about. When it happened, I set another goal, a reasonable, manageable goal that I could realistically achieve if I worked hard enough."
~Michael Jordan

MANAGE YOUR FINANCIAL AID

In this chapter, you will:
- Learn that part of your money management in college involves managing your financial aid.
- Confirm how much it costs for the educational program you're aiming for.
- Understand how you get financial aid and about some of the common and not-so-common sources of money for college.
- Analyze the financial aid packages being offered to you in order to choose the best deal.
- Know that financial aid can be crucial to attaining your goals.

YOU'LL NEED TO MANAGE YOUR FINANCIAL AID

Part of managing your money in college involves paying for college and your expenses while you're there. You need to learn to manage your financial aid. As you are probably quite aware, financial aid can be a confusing maze, but it is essential to your being able to reach your goals. It's one more thing you need to learn about and navigate through.

Keep a couple of basic things in mind:
- Some people can make you believe that college is very, very expensive and out of your reach. This is *not* true.
- Minority and underrepresented students *do* have a better chance at getting financial aid.
- The *earlier* you complete applications and forms, the more money you will probably get.

As you've discovered, different colleges cost different amounts. How much your college education costs depends on the type of program or college you choose. In some ways choosing your college is a bit like shopping for anything else. You will want to see if the school has the type of features you want and see what the bill will be. But whereas you have to pay for store-bought items all by yourself, you will most likely have help when paying for college.

Since you and your family are responsible for financing your college education, you should sit down together to compare costs at different colleges, keeping in mind *all* of the things you'll require in order to get an accurate total cost:

113

- tuition and fees
- books and supplies
- room and board (if you go away to school)
- transportation
- personal expenses, such as clothes, laundry, snacks, entertainment, phone, etc.

Don't make the mistake of looking only at tuition and fee expenses. While tuition and fees usually make up the largest percentage of total college cost, the other items contribute substantially.

Assignment #24

What will your college cost?

For the colleges or training programs you are most interested in, find out the following costs and write them down. (These should be for one year, not per semester.)

College/Program #1: _____
Tuition and fees   _____
Room and board (if you plan to live at school) _____
Books $800 (average)
Approximate transportation costs   _____
Personal expenses (snacks, stamps, phone cards) $750 (average)

                              Total _____

College/Program #2: _____
Tuition and fees   _____
Room and board (if you plan to live at school) _____
Books $800 (average)
Approximate transportation costs   _____
Personal expenses (snacks, stamps, phone cards) $750 (average)

                              Total _____

College/Program #3: _____
Tuition and fees   _____
Room and board (if you plan to live at school) _____
Books $800 (average)
Approximate transportation costs   _____
Personal expenses (snacks, stamps, phone cards) $750 (average)

                              Total _____

HOW DO I GET FINANCIAL AID? THE FAFSA IS THE KEY

The process to determine who qualifies for financial aid and how much each receives starts with you and your parents filling out the FAFSA (Free Application for Federal Student Aid) form. Hopefully, you have already completed and sent in this form. The FAFSA is required for most forms of financial aid--federal or state grants, federal loans, and work-study assistance. In addition, every college requires it if you are going to be requesting financial aid.

You cannot fill it out until January of your senior year in high school. Then it becomes available online or in your counselor's office. Once it becomes available you should complete it as soon as possible because this starts the ball rolling on financial aid. A key part of the FAFSA is the "need analysis." This asks for income information directly from your parents' tax return for that year, so it is essential that your parents complete their tax return as soon as possible.

The completed FAFSA is sent to a national agency for analysis. When they have completed their analysis and determined how much financial aid you are eligible for, they send you a SAR (Student Aid Report). The SAR gives you a number that represents your financial need by taking total college costs and subtracting student and parent contributions.

FINANCIAL AID OFFICES AT COLLEGES ARE CRUCIAL—GET TO KNOW YOUR FINANCAIL AID ADVISER

Once you have gotten college acceptance letters and are trying to decide which college to go to, a great deal of help can be obtained from the colleges' financial aid offices. They hold the key to paying for your education. The colleges will look at your financial need figure to determine how much financial aid you will require to attend their schools. (It's important to understand that your contribution and that of your parents is based on the federal need analysis formula from the FAFSA, not what you and your parents *think* can be contributed toward your education.)

The financial aid office knows about and distributes funds from a variety of sources. They will look at your financial need and package financial aid around it. In determining your "financial aid package," the colleges check to see if you're eligible for assistance from federal, state and college sources, and they will help you get that money. Your financial aid packages may include scholarships, grants, work-study, and/or loan assistance.

Get to know the financial aid adviser assigned to your particular case. Let him or her know the specifics about your particular situation. By being friendly, respectful, and helpful in providing information, you might get him or her to dig a little deeper to provide more aid.

A typical financial aid package is a combination of money from several sources. These sources and types of financial aid are:
1. **Grants**—free money you do not have to work for (except to keep your grades up) and you do not have to repay.
    a) Grants come from the federal government.
        - Pell Grant

- Supplemental Educational Opportunity Grant (SEOG)
- Academic Competitiveness Grant (ACG)

b) Grants also come from your state government.
- In D.C.—Tuition Assistance Grant (TAG) and Leveraging Educational Assistance Program (LEAP)
- In Maryland—Guaranteed Access Grant (GA) and Educational Assistance Grant (EA)

1. **Scholarships**— free money you do not have to work for (except to keep your grades up) and you do not have to repay. Scholarships can come from a variety of sources—your college, organizations, churches, employers, and private individuals.

2. **Work study**—Money you earn by doing some sort of work on campus.

3. **Loans**—Money you have to repay with interest after you graduate.

Examine the sample financial aid packages on the following pages.

Example of a Financial Aid Package

Two-Year College (such as Montgomery College, Prince George's Community College or Northern Virginia College)

Total Expenses for One-Year

Educational costs usually eligible for financial aid:
Tuition	$4600
Fees	$1000
Room and Board	NA
Books	$800
Total	$6400

Costs you usually pay out of your pocket:
Transportation (commute)	$1280
Personal (lunch on campus, etc.)	$650
Total	$1930

Financial Aid Package Offered for One Year

Total Educational Costs $6400
Expected Family Contribution (EFC) - 800
(The amount your family will be expected to pay will be determined by the FAFSA application. This is not what you and your family *think* you can pay, but what the government determines you can pay, based on a formula.)

Financial Need (minus the EFC) $5600

Pell Grant   -3800

Tuition Assistance Grant   -1250

Stafford Student Loan   -550 (Note the size of the loan, which you will be responsible for paying when you graduate, not your parents. It is likely you will have to borrow *about* this same amount of money each year you attend this school.)

Total Educational Costs   **0**

Total out-of-pocket expenses: $1930

Scholarship from your church   -850
Total out-of-pocket costs   **$1080**
you will need to pay

Another example of a Financial Aid Package

Private Four-Year College (such as Trinity, Spelman, Howard, Alleghany, etc.)

Total Expenses for One-Year

Educational costs usually eligible for financial aid:
Tuition		$14,000
Fees		$2500
Room and Board		$8450
Books		$800
	Total	$25,750

Costs you usually pay out of your pocket:
Transportation (bus or plane to & from campus)		$1500
Personal (laundry, phone, etc.)		$750
	Total	$2250

Financial Aid Package Offered for One Year

Total Educational Costs	$25,750
Expected Family Contribution (EFC) -	800

(The amount your family will be expected to pay will be determined by the FAFSA application. This is not what you and your family *think* you can pay, but what the government determines you can pay, based on a formula.)

Financial Need (minus the EFC)	$24,950
Pell Grant	-3800
Tuition Assistance Grant	-1250
Need-based grant from your college	-3500
Work-study	-1000
Stafford Student Loan	-15,400 (Note the size of the loan, which you will be responsible for paying when you graduate, not your parents. It is likely you will have to borrow *about* this same amount of money each year you attend this school.)
Total Educational Costs	**0**
Total out-of-pocket expenses:	$2250
Scholarship from your church	-850
Total out-of-pocket costs you will need to pay	**$1400**

...after Graduation

It's obvious that there is a huge difference in what you will pay (and what you will owe when you graduate) going to a two-year state school versus a private college or university. Four-year state schools, such as Delaware State, Morgan State, and University of Maryland, are somewhere in between the costs you see on the previous pages. As we have said, it pays to shop around. Check if the college offers the program you want, see how much it costs, and look for the best deal in terms of the financial aid package they offer.

Just as there is a wide range of prices for higher education and there is also a wide range of what colleges can offer in terms of financial aid. If you have acceptances from several colleges, part of you and your family's decision-making about which college to attend should involve the financial aid package you've been offered.

The financial aid package will most likely assist with the "cost of attendance." This includes tuition, fees, books, room and board, but often, personal expenses, such as transportation and money for laundry, snacks, phone, etc. are totally your responsibility. This is why it's a good idea to have a "college fund"—by saving money from summer or after-school jobs or that family members contribute to.

Assignment # 25

What is your best financial aid deal?

If you have acceptance letters and financial aid package award letters from any of the schools you have applied to, analyze which one will give you the best deal. Keep in mind that one school might be offering you the most money, but if their costs are the highest, then this might not be the best "deal."

College/Program #1: _____
Does this school have the program I want?	☐ Yes	☐ No
Does this school have the location I want?	☐ Yes	☐ No
Do they have the other things I'm looking for in a college?	☐ Yes	☐ No
Have they offered me an attractive financial aid package?	☐ Yes	☐ No

How much will my family and I have to pay for educational expenses after all the financial aid has been deducted from my costs? (This includes loans.)
_____

How much will my family and I have to pay for personal expenses?
_____

How much in total expenses (educational and personal) will my family and I will be paying each year?

Total_____

College/Program #2: _____
Does this school have the program I want? ☐ Yes ☐ No

Reach for College!

Does this school have the location I want? ☐ Yes ☐ No
Do they have the other things I'm looking for in a college? ☐ Yes ☐ No
Have they offered me an attractive financial aid package? ☐ Yes ☐ No
How much will my family and I have to pay for educational expenses after all the financial aid has been deducted from my costs? (This includes loans.)
_____

How much will my family and I have to pay for personal expenses?
_____

How much in total expenses (educational and personal) will my family and I will be paying each year?
Total_____

College/Program #3: _____
Does this school have the program I want? ☐ Yes ☐ No
Does this school have the location I want? ☐ Yes ☐ No
Do they have the other things I'm looking for in a college? ☐ Yes ☐ No
Have they offered me an attractive financial aid package? ☐ Yes ☐ No
How much will my family and I have to pay for educational expenses after all the financial aid has been deducted from my costs? (This includes loans.)
_____

How much will my family and I have to pay for personal expenses?
_____

How much in total expenses (educational and personal) will my family and I will be paying each year?
Total_____

NEED MORE MONEY?

After you've done the analysis of the financial aid package being offered to you and the college's costs, it is not unusual to be in the position of wanting to go to a school that seems too expensive for you. There are several things you can do.

First, you can appeal for more money. If a certain college is your first choice but it looks out of your reach financially, call the college and speak to your financial aid adviser. Colleges like to know they are a student's first choice, and if money is the only thing preventing a student from attending, sometimes the adviser can offer a slightly better package. It's worth a try.

Second, you can appeal by writing a letter to the financial aid office detailing a specific hardship or special circumstance and asking for more assistance.

Third, think about attending a more affordable college for one or two years and then transferring to your first choice college. This is a smart strategy because all first-year students take pretty much the same basic courses no matter what college they attend. You can be saving money while you're getting the basic courses (math, English composition, science, and social studies) out of the way and then transfer to your first-choice college when you start doing work in your major. This method can save you a great deal of money.

Fourth, don't forget to help yourself. Do your research so you are knowledgeable about other sources of money the college or financial aid office might not regularly think about. For example, if you are intending to major in certain areas, such as science, math, languages or computer sciences, these are considered nationally important areas because we need people trained in these fields. Tell your financial aid adviser you are intending to major in one of these fields because there are special programs and scholarships just for these fields. (One such new program is called the National SMART grant.) If you are interested in special education, nursing, gerontology, and many other fields, there are programs whereby your loans can be cancelled after you graduate if you work in those fields (check out the Stafford Service-Cancelable Loans.) If you have taken AP classes and pursued a rigorous high school program you might be eligible for an Academic Competitiveness Grant. The point is it literally pays to educate yourself about the opportunities out there. Start by looking at the federal government financial aid website; then look at your state's website.

- Federal government: http://studentaid.ed.gov (Check out things on the home page for new programs, then click the tab on "Funding".)
- District of Columbia: http://seo.dc.gov (Click on "Higher Education Financial Services")
- Maryland: http://www.mhec.state.md.us/ (Click on "Student Financial Assistance")

Fifth, there are scholarships. It can be a lot of work to research and apply for scholarships, but sometimes the pay-off is worth it. If you set a goal of sending out, say one application a week, you just might get two or three scholarships. These can add up and ease your life considerably. Two websites to look at, where you can do scholarship searches, are:

www.fastweb.com

www.finaid.com

You will probably have a better chance at getting local scholarships rather than national ones. The reason is simple: the applicant pool is smaller, so there's less competition. So, begin your scholarship search close to home. Here are some suggested places to look.

- Your high school guidance office bulletin board often lists local or special scholarships that might be right for you. Also ask your guidance counselor if he or she has a scholarship file you can look through. Counselors get lots of scholarship material sent to them, but can't process it all or put it all up on the bulletin board, so they might have a file.
- Your high school itself might offer scholarships that alums or local businesses sponsor just for your school. Ask your guidance counselor or person who specializes in scholarships.
- Parents' employers sometimes offer special scholarship programs for children of employees. Ask your parents to check with the Human Resources office at their place of employment.
- Your employer may offer scholarships for employees. More employers are aware of the increasing cost of college attendance and are offering college scholarships. Check with your supervisor.
- Your church might offer scholarships for youth members. Talk to someone who would know.

- Local businesses and civic organizations (such as the Rotary Club) may also have scholarship programs. Check the local paper, grocery store bulletin boards, or businesses you frequent, etc.

After you have exhausted all these possibilities then start to widen your search, but still restrict it somewhat to try to narrow the applicant pool. Here are some ways to restrict your search. Look for scholarships for students:
- Of certain ethnic or racial backgrounds.
- Interested in particular fields—for example, nursing, engineering, business, fire prevention, etc. There are hundreds of career-based scholarships.
- Who are members of a particular church denomination, such as Baptist, Methodist, etc.
- Who play a particular sport or instrument.
- Who have participated in student government or in other ways been a student leader.
- Who have participated in scouting, Boys and Girls Clubs, or other community-based organizations.
- Who have parents in the military or who were in the military previously.

One thing you should *never* do, however, is pay for a scholarship search. These are scams!! *All* scholarship information is free and is out there for anyone to search for. People who you pay to do scholarship searches are not going to come up with anything more than you can come up with yourself. There is no secret source of scholarships that only they know about, so don't get taken in!

IS IT SMART TO TAKE OUT A LOAN TO PAY FOR COLLEGE?

Yes, it is smart to take out a loan to invest in yourself and your future. Remember that every dollar you pay toward your education now will come back to you in ten and twenty dollar bills for the rest of your life. Also, you don't have to repay student loans until you graduate and the repayment terms are usually stretched out over a long period of time, so as not to cause a hardship for you as you're just starting out in life.

At the same time, it's also important to realize several things about student loans. If you quit school or don't graduate, you still have to repay the loan. You, not your parents, are responsible for repaying the loan. And if you make your payments late or do not repay the loan for some reason, this will adversely affect your credit report for a very long time.

So take out a student loan for the minimum amount of money you need and be sure to read all the fine print before signing on the dotted line. And then, study hard so you can make the most of your investment.

WILL I BE GIVEN THE SAME AMOUNT OF FINANCIAL AID AUTOMATICALLY EVERY YEAR OF COLLEGE?

You must re-apply every year.
You have to reapply for financial aid every year. But this is not as hard as it sounds. It is a hassle, but hey it's free money. And after you've been through the process once (this year) it won't seem so hard the next time around because you will be familiar with it.

If your financial circumstances are basically the same each year, then your financial aid package will, likely, stay about the same, or the amount you receive might increase. As we mentioned, there is a lot of money out there for students majoring in certain fields, so once you declare your major, more financial aid might open up to you.

The most important thing to remember about re-applying is to re-apply early. Since most institutions have limited resources, it's best to be early in the line to ask for them. You're more likely to get them and get a bigger piece of the pie.

You must keep your grades up.

If your grade point average falls below 2.0 you will lose your eligibility for financial aid. At that point you and your family would be totally responsible for paying for the full costs of your education. So, it is critically important that you do everything you can to study hard and keep your grades up.

OBTAINING FINANCIAL AID IS A CRITICAL PART OF THE PROCESS OF MOVING TOWARD YOUR GOALS

The whole process to obtain financial aid can seem difficult and tiresome. First, your family has to reveal its financial secrets, which no one likes to do. Second, you have to trust the government and the college with these secrets. Third, you're asking for someone to help you and yet they sort of have you over a barrel. No one likes to feel that someone else has control over his or her destiny. And yet, in order to reach your goals, you have to get past these things.

Keep these facts in mind. The *majority* of college students request and receive financial aid. The money has been put aside out of the taxes you and your parents have been paying all these years, to enable students to attend college, which is very expensive. It's time for you to get your share back now. Yes, the government will have all your financial information, but they already have it. By sending in tax forms every year, the government already knows your business. And the college will get your financial information, but they handle thousands of these a year. They will handle yours just like everyone else's—with professionalism and integrity. Trust them.

Send in your forms. Apply for all the money you can get. Do everything as early as you possibly can. Select the best deal for you. And move on toward you future with dignity and self-confidence.

"Knowledge is the key that unlocks all doors. It doesn't matter what you look like or where you come from if you have knowledge."
~Benjamin Carson

Chapter Nine

"Success is within your grasp. If you believe it is possible, you can make it happen. If you decide to become negative and believe that things will never be right, you will also have those results. So, be very careful what thoughts you put into your mind. For good or bad, they will boomerang right back to you."
~Beatryce Nivens, Beating the Odds, Success Strategies for African Americans

CREATE A "SUCCESS NETWORK" FOR YOURSELF

In this chapter, you will:
- Understand that success in your life from now on is your responsibility.
- Know that you will be more likely to succeed if you create a network of people you can lean on when things get hard.
- Learn that there are campus resources to help you with every challenge you might face at college.
- Practice learning about campus resources at the college you plan to attend.
- Think of other people/mentors you can lean on when the going gets tough.

YOUR SUCCESS IS YOUR RESPONSIBILITY

When you go off to college, whether you go across the city or across the country, your success is going to be your responsibility. You have to decide from day one that you intend to succeed in every class, make every transition, graduate and pursue your career goals with all your determination. You might have supporters or detractors behind you, but all the strength and perseverance has got to come from you now.

You will find it's not all hard work and struggle. College is a wonderful time to explore new opportunities, new ideas, new people and get to know yourself better too. It's fun and exciting! It's mind-expanding and eye-opening to get out of your comfort zone, to walk into new worlds and to have new thoughts. You will end up being a bigger person for it.

But there will also be challenges. Challenges might come in many forms, as you know. They can be academic, social, emotional or all three at once. You need folks to watch your back. You need a network!

LEAN ON ME

You know the old Bill Withers song. "Lean on me when you're not strong and I'll be your friend, I'll help you carry on." In everyone's life there come times when we need to lean on someone. Maybe your financial aid isn't arriving on time; you might need to lean on your financial aid adviser for help for a minute. Maybe your boyfriend at home is upset and wants you to come back home; you might need to lean on your roommate for advice and strength. Maybe your chemistry professor said something that got on your nerves; you might need to go lean on her for help and talk through why you're not doing so well in that class.

The point is that, sooner or later, everyone needs to lean on someone for support or help. What you need to do in order to give yourself the greatest chance at success is to start to build a support network as soon as you get to campus. You might say, "Well, okay, but I don't even know a soul on that campus yet." That's true. But the college has thought of that.

Every college knows that every student needs help sometime or other. The college *wants* you to succeed, so they have set up all kinds of helpful services just for you. (In fact, you're *paying* for these services with your student fees. So why not use them?) All you have to do is go look for them, then go in and introduce yourself to the kind people inside. And lo and behold, you will have started your network!

COLLEGES MAKE MANY RESOURCES AVAILABLE TO STUDENTS. USE THEM!

Colleges understand that students might need assistance. As a few examples, students might need help with:
- Getting all their financial aid in place.
- Succeeding in classes, with study habits, having enough time to get everything done.
- Adjusting socially to college-life—making friends, feeling homesick, living in a dorm.
- Health or mental health related issues—illnesses, depression.
- Home-related issues that are pulling you toward home.
- Personal issues—relationship problems, experiencing racism, making important decisions.

Whatever the problem (even if it's not listed here) it is *extremely* important to understand that you can get assistance with it on campus, and not just from your friends. Even though, at times, you might feel very alone with your problem or problems, it is highly likely that other students have experienced the same thing and the campus has resources already set up and waiting for you to use to help you with this issue.

The main thing is to build a network of people you trust in the offices and various campus centers and ask for assistance when you need it. **Remember to keep always in mind that your college *wants* you to succeed. They don't want you to go home or to drop out. They want you to continue to reach your goals, and they want to help you to do that. That is the *whole* reason they exist!** So, believe it when we say that they are already set up, somewhere on campus to help you. You just have to find the correct place or person.

Reach for College!

One way to find the correct place or person is by asking. Don't be shy. Don't be afraid. Swallow your pride. Yes, you are independent and smart and can handle things on your own. **But also keep in mind that it is actually a sign of strength and maturity to recognize that you are experiencing some difficulty and you are willing to ask for help** because this demonstrates that you are willing to do what it takes to succeed. **This demonstrates your grit and determination. Winners don't give up; they find a way even when the way seems hard or impossible. Smart people ask for help to make** *sure* **they succeed.**

Below are some examples of difficulties you might run into and where you might look for help. Keep in mind that if you run into a brick wall at one place, then try the next one and the next one. Remember that all people are only human, and we all have bad days sometimes. You might not get the help you expect from the first place you go. That's okay. That person might be having a bad day. Try the next resource on the list. Don't give up!!

Difficulty with financial aid:
- Financial aid office (and follow what they suggest you do)
- Your adviser
- Minority Affairs/Multicultural office
- An older student who's been through it
- Reach for College! adviser
- A family member

Not understanding things in a class/getting poor grades in a class:
- Your professor (Hint: Don't just talk to your professor after class. Make an appointment and have specific questions ready when you go talk to him/her. Explain what you don't understand or the difficulty you're having with the class. Be prepared to listen and take notes on how to improve.)
- Go to tutoring/resource center for help **often**!
- Organize a study group of other students from the class, or join an existing one
- Your adviser
- Minority/Multicultural affairs office
- See what resources are available on campus to get a private tutor for free
- Reach for College! adviser

Adjustment to college life (this might include roommate problems, feeling alone, feeling overwhelmed and wondering what you've gotten yourself into, commuter issues, feeling that everyone else is happier and doing better than you are, feeling homesick and worried or sad):
- Student Counseling Center
- An older student who's been through it
- A friend who is encouraging and supportive
- Minority/Multicultural Affairs Office
- Your adviser
- Reach for College! adviser

Reach for College!

Health issues—illness or extreme sadness:
- Student health center
- Resident assistant in dorm
- Roommate or friend
- Reach for College! adviser

Home issues—family problems, worries about your family:
- Counseling Center
- Friend
- Minority/Multicultural Affairs Office
- Your family's social worker
- Reach for College! adviser

Personal issues—relationship problems, making important decisions, experiencing racism or discrimination:
- Your roommate or friends
- Your adviser
- Minority Affairs/Multicultural Office
- Reach for College! adviser

Every college is different in terms of the services they offer, who offers the services, and what they call them. You will also find that you click with certain people in certain offices or centers and not with others. Maybe you've tried going to your adviser a couple of times and have found him to be too busy, pretty unsympathetic, and unhelpful each time. Fine. Move on. Find someone else you can talk to and who you feel gives you good suggestions. The important point is not to give up easily, but to keep seeking help until you get what you need to help you through whatever difficulty you're having.

Assignment # 26

What services are available at the college you're probably going to attend?

Who can you lean on at the college you're probably going to attend? Go to the website of the college you are planning to go to and look around to discover where you would go and what you would find there if you were experiencing the following difficulties.

1. Problems with your writing in your English 101 Composition class

I'd seek help at: _____

They offer these services that would probably be helpful in this situation _____

_____

2. Problems with keeping up in your Math 100 class

...after Graduation

I'd seek help at: _____

They offer these services that would probably be helpful in this situation _____

_____

3. Feeling sad and disoriented, missing home

I'd seek help at: _____

They offer these services that would probably be helpful in this situation _____

_____

4. Looking for things to do to be able to connect with people and make friends

I'd seek help at: _____

They offer these services that would probably be helpful in this situation _____

_____

5. You're starting to doubt your idea of the kind of career you want to pursue. Where can you go to find out about careers?

I'd seek help at: _____

They offer these services that would probably be helpful in this situation _____

_____

ESTABLISH RELATIONSHIPS WITH FACULTY, ADMINISTRATORS AND MENTORS

One of the surest paths to success in college is by establishing relationships with faculty members, administrators and potential mentors in your field. These people will also be part of your network. As we said earlier, everyone at a college is an adult. You are just younger and less experienced than the adults on the faculty. But they have chosen this profession because they *like* to help younger adults on their way to their goals in life, so let them help you.

Members of the administration and faculty *want* to feel a personal connection to students, just as you should want to feel a personal connection to faculty members. As you attend your classes and interact with people at the college, be on the lookout for people you feel comfortable with or with whom you seem to feel a connection. This might be because of their outlook—how they view the world that is similar to yours—or because of their personality—something about them that you like. And then make it a point to get to know them more and to let them get to know you. Be respectful of their time constraints, but also be friendly.

Make an appointment and go talk to them during their office hours. Talk to them about a class, either about some problem you're having in a class, or about an extension of some discussion in a class that you wished could have been talked about more. They will appreciate your thoughtful remarks and you should listen carefully to theirs too.

It is from these types of conversations that you will feel a greater connection to your new school and to the academic world you're entering. You will gain a greater understanding of the topic of your classes. And as you move into classes in your major, you will come to comprehend better, through your conversations, the career choices the major can lead to.

A faculty or administrator who is a friend/mentor can be helpful to you in times of difficulty. And they can certainly give you advice on the way toward your goals just because they have more experience of how things work on campus and in the world. Listen to their suggestions and act on them. This will often provide you with a short-cut and will greatly help you to be successful. When you get to college in your first couple of weeks, start a mental list of potential mentors and then follow up by talking to them, starting a connection.

JUMP ON PROBLEMS AS SOON AS YOU NOTICE THEM. DON'T WAIT.

Okay, say you've got the beginnings of a network of people you like and who like you, who you think you can call on if things get rough. Then two weeks into the first semester you realize that things aren't going so well in your science class because you don't understand the reading and there is so much of it! You've picked up a nasty cold and can't sleep. And, oh, the financial aid office is bugging you because they need one more piece of paperwork. What do you do?

Too often what students do is bury their heads under their pillows and hope everything will be better when they wake up. That strategy won't work. Or, they throw themselves into partying to "relieve the stress." That strategy won't work either. A big key to success in college is jumping on problems as *soon* as they arise. If you wait, it only gets worse. And it gets worse very fast.

You've got to ask for help the *minute* you see or feel something's going downhill because once it's on that slope, it's not going to stop sliding unless you do something to stop it. Get yourself to the health center and get something for your cold. Don't ignore the financial aid office—they hold the key to your money. Why would you jeopardize your money? And try the science reading one more time. If it still isn't making sense, make an appointment right away to talk to your science teacher. Maybe she will have suggestions of how to approach the reading. Maybe she will suggest another class and it's not too late yet to drop her class and add another one.

The point is: things won't improve unless you actively and aggressively pursue a course to make them improve. You've got to be self-aware to keep on top of how things are going in all areas of your life, in all of the transitions to college. And you've got to be ready to fix things

right away that might be slipping. If you wait, it will only make it harder to fix the problems and you will lose precious time going backwards that you could be going forwards.

So, help yourself to success. Be aware of problems while they're still small and work to reverse the trend. Use your network to help you succeed!

"You have to know you can win. You have to think you can win. You have to feel you can win."
~Sugar Ray Leonard

Chapter Ten

"Go in there and do the best you can."
~Tiger Woods

TIPS FOR STUDENTS WHO ARE WORKING, COMMUTERS OR PARENTS

In this chapter you will:
- Recognize your special needs if you are a student who is working, a commuter or a parent.
- Learn some tips for success especially for you.

CHALLENGES FOR STUDENTS WHO ARE WORKING, COMMUTING OR PARENTING

Colleges, unlike high schools, often have a highly diverse student body. There are all kinds of students on all kinds of schedules studying at colleges. Some are full-time, on-campus students. Some are part-time, commuting students. Many have jobs in addition to their roles as students. These jobs can be on or off campus. And some students have children. So, if you work and go to school, if you commute and live in an apartment or at home, or if you have children, you will not be viewed as unusual or less than the ideal student at your college. You will, however, face challenges that other students might not face.

In all of these cases—working, commuting, parenting—you will tend to feel less connected to the college and will likely feel the stress of your other time commitments more than students who don't have these other responsibilities. This is never a reason to give up on college, but it is a reason to understand why you may be feeling more stressed than other students.

When you have heavy responsibilities outside of your classes this can detract from your ability to give your full attention to college. Your hours away from school are probably spent in one or more of your other responsibilities and not in leisure time. So, it's likely that you feel overwhelmed and maxed out a lot of the time.

If you feel you can handle all this, then go for it. Of course, if you are not handling everything as well as you like, it's probably a good idea to cut back on something—either the number of classes you're taking or the number of hours you're working. Either way, you know that in order to keep your financial aid, you need to maintain a 2.0 GPA, so don't sacrifice your college money, if you can help it.

If you have children, most likely, you feel a special pull because you want to be able to spend as much time with them as you can and to be assured that they are being well cared for. But you also know that one of the best things you can do for them to be able to provide for them in long run is to get your education. So, you are being tugged strongly in many directions.

TIPS FOR SUCCEEDING AT COLLEGE WHILE YOU'RE WORKING, COMMUTING OR PARENTING

All of the suggestions in this book of how to succeed in college and of all the transitions to be aware of apply to you as well as to all other new college students, of course. So, use them to your advantage as you also find efficient ways to get everything done.

But here are a few more tips that apply just to you who have other responsibilities outside of school and/or are commuting to class:

Try to get connected to the school in some way.
Socially or academically, get involved at the school. This will probably be the most important factor to help you continue your studies. Don't think this is wasted time. It is your network and your connection to the school that will keep you going when time gets scarce or when you get discouraged.

Know your limits.
It doesn't do you any good to take four or five classes and work 40 hours a week at the same time. There just aren't enough hours in a day. Either you are going to fail some classes or your boss is going to be mad at you. If you absolutely have to work 40 hours per week, then drop back to taking two or three classes per semester. You will enjoy them more and you're life will be calmer. Yes, it might take you longer to graduate, but you also won't have a lot of F's on your transcript.

Meet with other students like you at school.
Are you a commuter? See if there is a message board for commuters or if a group for commuters exists. You can get to know one another and share your common experiences. This is all part of making connections at school.

Are you a parent? Talk to other parents. They might have tips about professors who are particularly lenient and helpful to students who are parents, who forgive your absences when your child is sick. There might be social groups specifically for parents to meet and mingle. These people can form the beginning of a network for you.

Use the services at your school.
Just because you might not be on campus as much as other students doesn't mean that you aren't entitled to the services the college offers students. In fact, there might be some services especially geared just for you, so find out about them. Is there a day-care center located on campus? If so, it probably has very reasonable rates and a good reputation. Are you feeling run-

down, overworked, and depressed? Don't forget that the Student Health Center is there for you. Want a place to work out? Your student fees pay for your access to the gym just like everyone else's. Take advantage of these things.

Stay in touch.
One of the hardest aspects of being a commuting, working, or parenting student is being tuned in to the news on campus. There is so much that happens every day on college campuses that it's just about impossible for everyone to keep up with it. But if you're only there a couple of days or evenings a week or you come just for your class and leave right afterward, it's sometimes difficult to be aware of changes, opportunities, and events that on-campus students find out about through word-of-mouth or by randomly placed posters.

You have to make a special effort to stay in touch with the communications from your college. How do they get the word out to you and most students? Is it on the website or one part of the website? Is it on one particular bulletin board? Is it through mailings? What ever is the method, you have to be sure to check it frequently. This can save you time and aggravation if classes have been moved or so you don't miss deadlines. But this can also provide you with opportunities. Maybe a recruiter is coming from a certain company or agency and you want to know about hiring there. Maybe a particular music group is coming to perform on campus and you would like to get tickets. Make sure you have heard about these things.

EVEN THOUGH IT'S CHALLENGING, DON'T GIVE UP

No one said it was going to be easy. If you're a commuting, working, or parenting student (or maybe all three) it's going to be tough. There's no doubt about that. College in itself is a challenge, especially the first year. And then you have taken on these other roles too that tend to make you feel alienated and disconnected from the academic life. It's hard.

But do whatever you can to stick with it. College, as you know, is your best shot for a better deal in life. It's your best shot for a better deal for your children too, so don't give up. Use all your resources and the school's resources to get through. Connect with people who can help you. Be determined and positive. You will reach the success you dream of. Just accept the challenge and do your best!

"You may encounter defeats, but you must not be defeated. In fact, it may be necessary to encounter the defeats, so you can know who you are, what you can rise from, how you can still come out of it."
~Maya Angelou

Reach for College!

INDEX

Academic calendar 17
Academic preparation 10-11, 63
Academic transition 33, 127
   academic/social life balance 26-28
   accept the challenge to succeed 35-36
   do the reading and writing on time 34
   focus on your goals 3-7, 35
   talk to your professor 35
   use campus resources 35
Active learner 41-44
Add/Drop 23
Administration Building 14
Adviser 12
Attitude for success 56-57
Banking 90-92
   banking forms 93-99
   banking vocabulary 92-93
   checking and savings accounts 90-91
Budget 87-89
Bursar 12
Calendars 17, 77-79
Career or Placement Center 15
Catalog 19
Class schedule 19, 21-22
College graduation 4, 17
Commuting student 133-135
Counseling Center 15
Credit cards 99-100
Credit reports 102,, 108-109
Credit/credit hour 16
Deans 12
Degree 15-17
Eat well 82-83
Emotional transition 59-67, 127
   depressed/overwhelmed 59, 127
   family issues 61-62, 128
   feel academically behind 63, 127
   feel out of place 63-65, 127, 128
   girlfriends/boyfriends 62-63, 127
   homesickness 60-61, 127
   new identity—who are you? 65-66, 127
   socially uncomfortable 63-65, 127
Family pulls and pressure 5, 61-62
Feeling out of place 63-65
Final exams 50-51
Financial aid 113-123
Financial aid management 113-123, 127
   FAFSA 115

   financial aid adviser 115-116
   financial aid package 115-119
   student loans 107-108, 116-119, 122
Focusing on goals 3-7
Friends 5, 29, 62-63, 127-128
Goals 3-7
Goal-setting 3-7
   focus on goals 3
   timeline to goals 7
Graduate student 17
Health Center 15, 128
   stay healthy 83-85
Homesickness 60-61
Incomes and educational levels 4
Independence 81-82
Instructor 13
Lecture 16
Loans 101-108
   car loans 101-104
   student loans 107-108
Major/declare a major 16
Mid-term exams 50-51
Minor/declare a minor 16
Money management 87-89
Network 125
Note taking 45-47
Parenting student 133-135
Placement tests 10-11
Pre-professional degree 17
Prerequisite 16
President and Vice-presidents 12
Professor 13, 35
   adjunct professor 13
   assistant professor 13
   associate professor 13
   full professor 13
Provost 12
RA (Resident Assistant) 13
Racism 64-65
Registrar 12
Registration 10, 19, 22
   add/drop 23
   catalog 19-20
   prerequisites 16
   schedule of classes 21-22
   your schedule 22
Relationships 5, 29, 62-63, 122-131
Responsibilities 81-112

eat well...82-83
health......................................83-85, 128
money..87-89
personal space/clothes 82
safety 85
Safety 85
Schedule of Classes........................ 19, 21-22
Seminar 16
Social transition 25-26
academic life/social life balance..............26-28
openness to new people and experiences.........29-30
your values....................................30-32
Student Union 14
Study Abroad 17
Study skills.. 36-52
improve focus 39-41
learning environment.............................37-39
note taking..45-48
organization skills...................................53
SQ3R 42-44
Syllabus...53-56
teacher clues 47
test taking..48-52

Stumbling blocks/not reaching goals...........5
Family...5
Fear...5
Friends..5
Job 5
tired of school 5
"Success Network" 125
Syllabus.. 53-56
TA (Teaching Assistant) 13
Test taking.. 48-52
Time balance 26-28
Time management....................26-28, 69-79
Calendars......................................17, 77-79
discipline/habit 76-77
plan 73
prioritize 71-73
routines 76-77
Tutoring (Center) 15
Undergraduate student 17
Values 30-32
Working student................................ 133-135